PRAISE FOR *HOW WE COULD*

"You can't resist reality, at least not for long. Circumstances aren't an excuse, they're context. This book shows you how to lead inside the mess, rather than waiting for the mess to clear."

—**Michael Bungay Stanier,** Author of *The Coaching Habit*, Over 1 million copies sold worldwide

"Effective communication breaks down the moment drama enters the room. Alex Dorr provides leaders with a practical, repeatable process to cut through the noise and coach their people to clarity and action. This is the framework modern teams have been missing."

—**Erica Dhawan,** Bestselling Author, Rated World's Top Female Speaker on Teamwork and Innovation

"Truly accountable leadership is the only way organizations survive and thrive. This book understands that deeply, and delivers a five-step framework that embeds accountability at every level, eliminates the drama that holds teams back, and ensures the next right action is always clear."

—**Dr. Vince Molinaro,** *New York Times* Bestselling Author, Founder & CEO of The Leadership Contract Inc.

"As trusted advisors, CPAs are expected to lead through complexity and deliver results under pressure. This book provides a very practical guide on building the kind of accountable, drama-free environment that can help accounting firms and their clients drive better alignment and more successful outcomes."

—**Erik Asgeirsson,** President & CEO, CPA.com, and Accounting Today Top 100 Most Influential People in Accounting

"In a profession dedicated to restoring function and movement, we know better than anyone that progress requires the right framework applied with consistency and care. This book brings that same discipline to leadership - a clear five step approach that gets teams aligned, accountable, and moving forward together."

—**Justin Moore,** CEO, American
Physical Therapy Association (APTA)

"This framework helped our teams create clarity, find their voice and step up in ways we had not seen before. A must read for any leader serious about building a culture where everyone contributes and delivers."

—**Curtis C. Simard** President & CEO, Bar Harbor Bank & Trust

"The work Alex did with our team gave every leader a clear playbook for any situation - no drama, no excuses, just a confident path forward. This book delivers that same impact at scale."

—**Tom Lowery,** Division President, Legrand

"Whether I'm building a championship esports roster or scaling a successful company, the formula is always the same - elite talent who embrace optimism and a positive culture equals extraordinary results. This book gives every leader that formula in five clear, powerful steps."

—**Mike "Hastr0" Rufail,** CEO & Owner of ENVY,
2024 Esports Awards Lifetime Achievement recipient

"In a world that delivers uncertainty on a daily basis, the approach in this book sets us up to be able to pivot and move when we face an unpreferred reality. It teaches us that we can and must succeed regardless of the circumstances."

—**Caroline Stockdale,** Chief People Officer, First Solar, Named 2025 Top People & Communications Officer

"I've led teams in some of the fastest-moving environments in business, and Alex's Reality-Based Leadership approach has been a go to resource for my leaders. *How We Could* takes that foundation and makes it even more actionable for the modern leader chasing big goals."

—**Kahly Berg,** Global Vice President, Digital Growth Marketing, SAP

"This framework fundamentally shifts how leaders and employees show up. It moves people out of blame and into ownership where reality isn't the problem, it's the opportunity. The result is teams that feel more in control, more accountable, and far more capable of driving real results."

—**Nickolett Hocking,** Senior Vice President of People, Angel City Football Club

"Hospitality is the ultimate people business - and drama is the enemy of delight. Alex's work and the approach in this book gave our teams a shared language, a clear framework and the confidence to coach through any challenge with empathy and conviction. It changed the way we lead and the way our guests experience us."

—**Jocelyn Blandford,** Director, Global Entertainment & Guest Experience, Carnival Cruise Line

HOW
WE
COULD

HOW WE COULD

THE FRAMEWORK *to*
LEAD WITHOUT DRAMA,
BUILD ALIGNMENT, *and*
CALL TEAMS *to* GREATNESS

ALEX DORR

FC
FAST
COMPANY
Press

Published by Greenleaf Book Group Press
Austin, Texas
www.gbgpress.com

Distributed by Greenleaf Book Group

For ordering information or special discounts for bulk purchases, please contact Greenleaf Book Group at PO Box 91869, Austin, TX 78709, 512.891.6100.

Design and composition by Greenleaf Book Group
Cover design by Greenleaf Book Group
Cover image used under license from ©Adobestock.com

Publisher's Cataloging-in-Publication data is available.

Print ISBN: 979-8-88645-516-8

eBook ISBN: 979-8-88645-517-5

To offset the number of trees consumed in the printing of our books, Greenleaf donates a portion of the proceeds from each printing to the Arbor Day Foundation. Greenleaf Book Group has replaced over 50,000 trees since 2007.

Printed in the United States of America on acid-free paper

26 27 28 29 30 10 9 8 7 6 5 4 3 2 1

First Edition

Just because I'm not the first to follow
doesn't mean that I can't feel it.
Just because it's been written in stone
doesn't mean that I can't complete it.

—MAXIMILIAN EUBANK

CONTENTS

INTRODUCTION: "I Can See It!" 1

PART I: LOVE PEOPLE UP

CHAPTER 1: CALL TO GREATNESS STEP 1.
Validate the Experience or Feelings 27

PART II: CALL PEOPLE UP

CHAPTER 2: CALL TO GREATNESS STEP 2.
Clean Up Thinking: The Edit Your Story Tool 47

CHAPTER 3: CALL TO GREATNESS STEP 3.
Find Your Part: The Accounting For Tool 71

CHAPTER 4: CALL TO GREATNESS STEP 4.
Know Your Role: The Organizational
Alignment and Buy-In Decision Table 95

PART III: ANSWER THE CALL

CHAPTER 5: The Situation, Background, Assessment,
and Recommendations (SBAR) Tool 135

CHAPTER 6: Thinking Inside the Box Tool 155

CHAPTER 7: Negative Brainstorming 185

CONCLUSION 213

ACKNOWLEDGMENTS 221

RESOURCES 225

INDEX 227

ABOUT THE AUTHOR 233

INTRODUCTION

"I CAN SEE IT!"

The day that sparked this book was supposed to be routine. Twenty regional directors from a major US retailer were gathered in New York City along with me—a leadership consultant with a growling stomach—as the tantalizing aroma of lunch preparations meandered through the air. Little did I know, this ordinary moment was about to fundamentally transform leadership thinking moving forward.

"Let's get practical," I said, fighting the urge to check my watch. "Think of a situation where you're facing resistance. Something drowning in 'Why we can't' or 'Why we shouldn't have to.' In other words, drama."

Before I could finish my sentence, the floodgates burst open. Instantly, the room surged with negative energy as a universal pain point emerged: the company's credit card sign-up initiative. Meant to be a key strategy to drive growth, it had become an initiative plagued by pushback, noncompliance, and dismal results.

Two years of nagging employees. Inconsistent execution. Some leaders soaring past targets, others barely lifting off the ground. And the kicker? A pervasive belief that offering credit cards was "too salesy" despite it being a top-priority strategy.

As I absorbed the information, I grabbed a flip chart, drew a box, and began creating a visual to move from discussion to action. At the top of the box, I scribbled, "GOAL: OFFER CREDIT CARD SIGN-UPS TO CUSTOMERS."

"What is currently getting in the way of staff offering these cards?" I asked. "What challenges are you hearing or seeing out there?"

An onslaught of obstacles poured out:

"Our younger workers just don't like to sell."

"Some customers get upset when you offer them the credit cards."

"Machines are sometimes down in the stores, which makes it difficult to sign up interested customers."

"We have a staff shortage."

"Sometimes people don't show up for work."

"Clothes need to be folded, so there is no time."

"We're too busy."

"Some people just won't do what we tell them to do."

I wrote every challenge being shared on either side of the box.

Once the concerns were exhausted, I pointed at the flip chart, we took a collective deep breath, and I invited the group to reflect: "Given that the company has established this goal and given these real challenges your teams are facing, what ideas do you have for how we could move forward?"

Silence. Some stared blankly; others smirked—as if my question proved I didn't understand the complexity and messiness of the situation.

Finally, one of the leaders broke it by exclaiming, "I can see it!"

"You can see . . . what?" I asked, confused.

"I must come clean here," she said. "I have been zero compliant.

My team isn't even attempting to sell the credit cards, and for some reason, because you drew the situation that way and acknowledged what is challenging, I can see seven or eight things I *could* be doing to achieve that goal."

"Are you willing to share?" I asked.

She began, "I could clarify with my team that offering the credit cards is nonnegotiable. I could retrain them on the scripts and do role-playing to get them more comfortable offering the credit cards. I could quit making this initiative optional and stop colluding when my team complains. I could share our progress weekly, make it competitive, and show results across stores to reveal it's possible. I can create a backup plan for when machines are down."

As she spoke, she kept her gaze on the flip chart, as if reading ideas from inside the box though they weren't written there. Her body language transformed, and her spirit seemed lighter, more willing. Many of these ideas had been suggested before by colleagues and quickly disregarded by her and her team. Now, she jotted down her favorites and felt newfound energy to take action.

Over lunch, a final comment revealed the deeper insight: "I don't know why, but because you heard us out and wrote down every challenge, it provided relief because it showed you listened. Seeing it written down made the situation finally feel doable."

Although her leaders had insisted the initiative was an important business priority, until this exercise, she hadn't been persuaded. The visual representation flipped her energy and demeanor. She went from two years of entrenched resistance to clarity about what could be done and willingness to do it.

The visual tool didn't *solve* the problem. It *dissolved* the distractions and limiting beliefs that had led to excuses instead of results.

Following her insights, the rest of the team chipped in with additional ideas. This open-minded and talented group realized a powerful truth that is at the core of Reality-Based Leadership and embedded in the spirit of this book: **Your circumstances aren't the reason you can't succeed but the reality in which you must.**

The result? The leaders returned to their regions with newfound clarity and willingness. Nearly all groups reported full compliance less than two months later, and credit card sign-ups surged, boosting sales across the country. By embracing this profound shift, they succeeded in the face of challenging circumstances.

To say this experience stuck with me is an understatement. I spent months revisiting what allowed that group to move from completely stuck to seeing possibilities, and it hit me: Countless leaders face this exact situation every single day—problems to solve, people stuck on why they can't.

What if my approach—facilitating a shift from "why we can't" to "how we could"—was what leadership in the modern workplace was really about? That question became the inspiration for this book.

I've spent over a decade at Reality-Based Leadership (RBL) speaking and training with tens of thousands of leaders across the world. The mental patterns that lock teams into "why we can't" have emerged clearer than ever, and the breakthroughs from that day have echoed louder. I want to share these patterns with you and give you the tools to create the same shifts with your teams. My hope is to inspire you to start calling people to greatness.

The Alarming Trends in Leadership

With that experience hanging around in my mind, it became all-consuming when I read recent reports on the state of the global workplace and how leaders, as a whole, are doing.

In a 2025 investigation into workplace engagement, Gallup reported a shocking 73 percent of managers and 82 percent of individual contributors are quitting their jobs every single day.

The problem?

They keep coming to work and collecting a paycheck.

Did you catch the sneaky joke there? They have completely quit *mentally* in what Gallup calls active or passive disengagement.

This level of disengagement is estimated to cost the world economy $438 billion annually. A jaw-dropping 17 percent of individual contributors are actively disengaged, meaning they are not simply going through the motions; they are consciously working against the goals of their organization while still collecting resources.[1]

So how are managers doing?

The same report discovered that 70 percent of team engagement is attributable to the manager. This makes sense because where the manager goes, so goes the team.[2]

Deloitte's *2025 Global Human Capital Trends* reports that 36 percent of managers felt they were not sufficiently prepared for the people-management part of their role, and because of that, 40 percent of managers reported their mental health declined when they took on their leadership role.[3]

Reports show business change is rapidly accelerating, with most leaders looking for agile new ways of working while employees conversely hope for greater stability.

But Alex, at least we are working on the problem, right?

Hopefully, managers are seeing these trends and putting their time and energy in the right places.

The same Deloitte study reveals that 41 percent of managers are spending their time every day on work that doesn't contribute organizational value. Nearly 40 percent of manager time is consumed

---

1 Gallup, *State of the Global Workplace: Understanding Employees, Informing Leaders* (2025), https://www.gallup.com/workplace/349484/state-of-the-global-workplace.aspx.

2 Gallup, *State of the Global Workplace.*

3 Corrie Commisso et al., *2025 Global Human Capital Trends* (Deloitte, 2025), https://www2.deloitte.com/content/dam/insights/articles/glob187692_global-human-capital-trends/DI_2025-Global-Human-Capital-Trends.pdf.

by firefighting today's problems or administrative work. Eighty-two percent of managers recognize the importance of freeing up worker capacity, but only 8 percent report they're making great progress at it.

These same managers know they need the training and tools to provide clear, honest, and actionable feedback that helps workers grow, but only 54 percent say they're confident in coaching for career development.[4]

Stepping back to take this all in, it's apparent we've come to a point where managers are underprepared and ill-equipped to manage their teams, resulting in a workforce that is largely checked out and resistant to change, ultimately draining company resources and limiting growth.

It has become increasingly clear that our current approach to leadership simply isn't sustainable.

Our Work So Far

Over the last decade at RBL, we've been on a mission to redefine the role of a leader and have made tremendous headway in outlining a new approach to tackle these challenges.

Through our research and work with tens of thousands of leaders across industries, RBL uncovered that the average person was spending nearly two and a half hours per day in drama. This included behaviors such as arguing with reality, resisting change, venting, judging, sidestepping accountability, and lacking alignment with organizational decisions.

Drama is mental and emotional waste. Recapturing this time and energy lost to drama appeared to be the biggest business opportunity hidden in plain sight for organizations.

This discovery led us to put forward a bold new idea for the role of modern leaders: **What if leaders spend less time trying to**

4 Corrie Commisso et al., *2025 Global Human Capital Trends.*

continuously inspire, motivate, or engage their teams and instead focus on ditching the drama from the workplace?

In business, waste or inefficiency is improved by implementing good processes. The emotional waste of drama is improved by teaching, facilitating, and coaching with good *mental* processes. To support leaders in doing this, we combined our best mental process tools into a leadership toolkit that leaders could use to fulfill this role, and we began teaching these tools for the last decade in organizations across the world. As people used these tools to move their teams into good mental processes during their daily work, they experienced quickly the power of recapturing the two and a half hours lost to drama. They naturally started achieving greater business results and increased well-being. In other words, they started to see that a team's natural state once drama is gone is innovation, collaboration, engagement, accountability, results, and teamwork. Most important, these leaders realized that the more skillful someone is at navigating drama at work, the more inspired and motivated they feel.

But here's what else we discovered: **Having these great tools isn't enough. Leaders need a clear, repeatable way to use them.**

Over the past decade, as I've trained leaders across nearly all industries, from health care to banking, high-tech to financial services, manufacturing to the public sector, a pattern emerged. Weekly, we'd hear breakthrough testimonials on how these mental-process tools helped shift team mindsets and move people into possibilities after being stuck, sometimes for years, on business issues. Leaders loved the tools and saw their power firsthand.

Yet many struggled with knowing which tool to use when, or how to sequence them for maximum impact. Some would jump straight to problem-solving without validating their team's experience first, causing the tools to land as harsh or manipulative. Others would use one tool brilliantly but miss the fuller picture that came from a complete process.

With this in mind, I doubled down on teaching and sharpening not just the tools themselves but how to organize them into a coaching process that any leader could follow with confidence. I worked intensively with the more than 150 clients I engage with per year, as well as with our RBL internal team, testing and refining until we had a framework that felt natural, repeatable, and consistently effective. For our organization internally, this resulted in more than 20 percent growth in profitability using half the staff and with improvements in well-being and work–life balance.

In creating this book, I also worked to synthesize the insights from Reality-Based Leadership's nearly three decades of experience teaching leadership in many of the top companies in the world, and one big truth emerged: These visual tools are not just helpful; they are essential to effective leadership in today's workplace. They should be at the forefront of how leaders navigate situations that are snagged by drama. Here's the bottom line: **If leaders aren't using the RBL tools, they aren't ditching the drama. If leaders aren't ditching drama, they won't have a team that can consistently succeed in the face of challenges.**

These tools are secret weapons for leaders to hold space for thinking as teams search for solutions when facing less-than-ideal situations at work. But organized into an intentional framework, they become unstoppable.

Introducing The Call to Greatness Framework

Here's what you are going to learn in this book: a five-step coaching framework that integrates seven RBL visual tools to help you move any team member from "why we can't" to "how we could"—no matter what challenge they are facing.

Used on their own, each tool has shown the power to quickly create this shift, but when combined they form an intentional coaching framework that enables leaders to systematically defuse any situation immersed in drama, ambiguity, or resistance.

The Call to Greatness Framework is a simple five-step leadership approach to support you in making this happen in conversations, team meetings, and one-on-one coaching.

Step 1: *Validate the experience or feelings.*

Step 2: *Clean up thinking (about the issue).*

Step 3: *Find your part (in the situation).*

Step 4: *Know your role (in the solution).*

Step 5: *Take next right action.*

Ultimately, The Call to Greatness Framework is an *invitation* to an individual or team to question or reconsider the sense they're making of an experience that has them stuck. It's not a mandate. You can't explain or talk someone into a call to greatness.

The power of a leader isn't what you tell people; it's what you get them thinking about or reflecting on. For this reason, the framework is powered by self-reflection and facilitated through visual tools and reflection exercises at each step.

When Does This Framework Matter Most?

Leadership is just a title when you're operating in a preferred reality—when work is going smoothly and as planned. Some call this the flow state, others call it the zone. When your team is clear on what to do, executing with conviction and proceeding joyfully, you can essentially forget everything you're about to read in this book. My best advice?

Do absolutely nothing. Enjoy the moment. Sit back and absorb the performance as your metaphorical orchestra is in perfect harmony.

Where the framework becomes useful is when your team is experiencing what I call an unpreferred reality. You know: the other 98 percent of your day? Only kidding . . . I hope!

Unpreferred realities include the times when things don't go as expected, people experience disruptions, or another department drops the ball and a mess lands at your team's feet. These unpreferred realities are precisely where workplace drama begins if not approached intentionally.

Humans are often not rational, but we are predictable. As ingrained in the human condition, most people react to an unpreferred work reality in one of two unhelpful ways. First, they argue with the identified unpreferred reality (*Ain't it awful? Things shouldn't be this way. This shouldn't be happening. Who made this decision? This situation is ridiculous!*). Once that gets exhausting, they typically transition to wishing for a different ideal future in which someone swoops in to fix things or save the day (*If we had more people, more resources, different market conditions, competent leadership . . .*). Worse, in this wishing for a different future, they often take no action.

Being stuck in these two spaces is a colossal waste of precious energy that typically leads to chronic frustration, disengagement, and lackluster results.

To add insult to injury, people tend to step down in the very moment they could add the most value. In a hypothetical world of technological perfection, human intervention would be obsolete. Instead, **our value lies in navigating the imperfect, the unpredictable, and the chaotic**. Humans thrive where automation falters, where standardization breaks down, and where reliable processes fall short. In other words, the unpreferred reality is our call to jump in, not our excuse to fade out.

This is precisely where **leaders must become energy managers**. They invite their teams to the space (sometimes a tiny space) between an unpreferred reality and the ideal future they're hoping to create. This is the space for impact.

Visually, I find it best to view it like this:

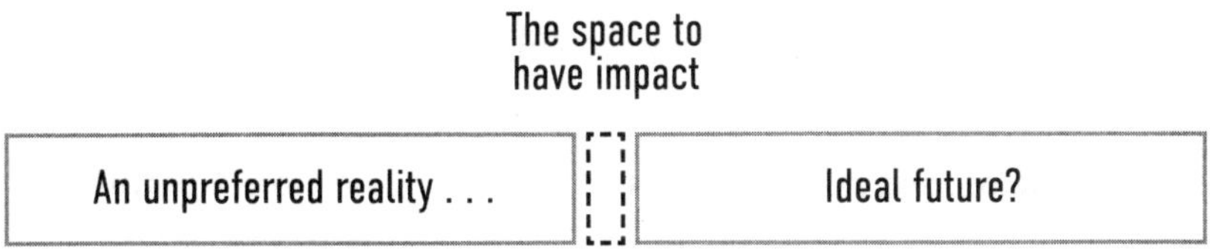

Whether it is fifty or five hundred times per day, leaders connect the unpreferred reality their team is facing to a different and better future. Leaders are the bridge builders between those two places. In that invitation, they also insist that the team doesn't just find the space but acts. Essentially, leaders are standing courageously with their teams and saying, **"Given this unpreferred reality, and in the spirit of the ideal future we're trying to create, how could we get there? Let's find the space for impact."**

If people sincerely reflect on that question, they are more empowered to engage and add value in the situation. This is where leaders live. If you use the ideas and tools of this book, you can consistently ensure that your team is stepping into that space as well.

Whether with your team, colleagues, board, leaders, external partners, or family members, this new skill set to get people to occupy that space is the essence of the call to greatness and how the most effective leaders are elevating their teams and evolving everyone they interact with. Essentially, when work doesn't feel effortless, or there's a sense of internal suffering, or you feel a lack of progress, it's a potential opportunity for The Call to Greatness Framework.

How to Use the Framework

The whole framework is greater than its parts. It's best to take an issue or challenge through the entire Call to Greatness Framework. Don't confuse initial clarity from one tool for the optimal clarity that the entire framework produces.

Many examples in this book are what I call touch-and-go coaching moments, when the first tool or first few reflections reveal next right action and you can quickly move forward. However, **the precise and ideal next right action will always come from the full Call to Greatness Framework** and completing all the reflection through the tools.

With limited time, you will always weigh the trade-offs of taking a few more minutes to complete the final steps. Exiting early always runs the risk of an unhelpful decision—aka taking next wrong action—because you don't have the full picture.

Luckily, next wrong action isn't ever *really* wrong in the end. It simply leads to learning new information and usually a new unpreferred reality that can be improved with another round through the framework. Nothing is lost because you can simply return to Step 1.

Otherwise, you might be tempted to skip the early steps and jump right to a tool that seems appropriate and faster to deal with the problem.

When clients began implementing these tools without the framework, it was comparable to playing the game Whac-A-Mole at the arcade.

This approach of seeing a source of drama and then smacking it with a tool that seemed best suited created initial momentum for many leaders and helped them feel the possibilities. However, **these tools in the wrong hands and used in the wrong spirit can come across as harsh**. This happens when someone skips the step of validating feelings or personal experiences and moves too quickly into problem-solving with their selected tool. Instead of facilitating an intentional and natural flow, this tactic can come across as rigid and robotic or, in the worst cases, manipulative.

If you find yourself accused of being harsh while using this framework or the approach seems to land flat with your team, check to see whether you are skipping any steps or rushing past Step 1. Breezing past the validation of someone's experience is a guaranteed way to get off on the wrong foot. Leadership moments are often nuanced, requiring a bit more finesse. A more helpful strategy is to use the tools together in an intentional framework that can help anyone, leaders and individual contributors alike, take any challenging situation at work and go through a series of simple steps to arrive at clarity and next right action.

With time and repetition, using the tools becomes second nature. You'll quickly become adept at running through the framework in a fluid way.

As your team becomes well-versed in the tools of The Call to Greatness Framework, it transforms from a structured sequence into a fluid practice. It begins to lose the rigidity of trying to decode a combination lock and resembles instead the intuitive approach of an expert physical therapist. Although the therapist may flow through their systematic assessment, they never skip a step, even when a client points directly to their pain. Why? Because they understand that what hurts isn't always the source of the *real* problem. A client might arrive convinced their hip is the issue, only for the therapist to discover the real culprit is a chain of tension points, beginning with a tight lower back pulling on the hip flexors and ending at shortened quad muscles, creating imbalance. Only by following this connected chain, pausing to release each knot fully before moving on, can one find lasting relief.

This mirrors exactly how increased fluency in The Call to Greatness Framework starts to play out. While someone might come to you certain they know where they're stuck, your role is to guide them sequentially through each step. Often, what seems like a struggle with knowing their role actually stems from unresolved tangles in their thinking or unacknowledged blind spots in their accountability. When you discover these stuck points or "knots," that's your signal to slow down and fully employ the reflection tool for that step until you notice that same kind of release.

Like a skilled therapist feeling when the knot finally dissolves, you'll know when it is time to move forward. The path to next right action begins to illuminate naturally unless, of course, you discover another knot that needs attention. Trust the framework, notice the tension points, and give each stuck point the time it needs to truly release.

Now, I want to address an obvious irony present in this book. Many of the stories you will read show the power and transformational possibilities of each *individual* tool and are essentially showing myself or other leaders doing the Whac-A-Mole approach to ditching drama that I've just said has been effective but not ideal.

This decision to feature the tools in that way was made for learning purposes, to support you as a reader so you can better understand each tool before bringing it all together within the full framework. That said, I've included a full Call to Greatness Framework example that threads through each chapter in the book to show you how the framework should be ideally used when you have the time and space to walk through all five steps.

Why the Tools Must Be Visual, Not Verbal

The RBL tools embedded in each step of the framework are inherently visual, a design choice that serves a dual purpose. While many individuals are visual learners who benefit greatly from graphical representations, there's a more scientific rationale behind this approach.

Visual tools in leadership serve as powerful cognitive scaffolds. They externalize our thought processes, allowing us to literally see our thinking. This visualization fundamentally alters how we engage with complex situations that are prone to drama.

A psychological phenomenon called projection often derails problem-solving in the workplace. Projection is the process of displacing one's feelings onto a different person, animal, or object. The term is most used to describe defensive projection, attributing one's own unacknowledged stress to another source. This happens when people begin to confuse their leaders with the problem they are trying to solve. A seemingly harmless request can become an absolute free-for-all of fear, speculation, resistance, and focus on "why we can't."

It's as if you dropped a pebble into a pond with a change request and expect a gentle ripple, but instead you are met with a tidal wave back as a response from your team. This is the feeling that often accompanies this dynamic in the workplace, and it's precisely what visual tools help to prevent. By externalizing the problem on paper, the issue becomes objective rather than personal.

Byron Katie, author of *Loving What Is*, is among my favorite teachers about stress and how it affects one's life. She often says, "All war belongs on paper." In her work, she is referring to the mental war the ego plays in disrupting happiness. However, the same is true when you are leading people through challenges they don't love at work.

It's difficult to simply think your way through to the best next action. That "war" also belongs on paper. Immersed in ambiguity and endless discussion, the problem can hide out in lack of accountability. When commitments aren't written down, there is no tangible follow-up action to hold anyone accountable to.

The RBL tools embedded in The Call to Greatness Framework help put the issue to metaphorical paper (or, in virtual settings, a spreadsheet, PowerPoint slide, or shared screen) to clean up thinking, help people take accountability for their space for impact, and move into next right action. The problem no longer has a place to hide in the fog of ambiguity that leads to situations that feel impossible to figure out. Most important, the framework makes the issue conscious and visible to everyone so that the team can get intentional about what to do about it.

Together, standing side by side and supporting each other, you can solve the challenges your organization faces. It's not us versus them, leaders versus staff, or you versus me. It never has been. It's us versus an unpreferred reality trying to prevent us from achieving our goal. Given that, what would great look like, and what's our first step to get there?

This breakthrough occurs when enough cognitive friction has been generated by holding the center with the tools while people continue thinking about possibilities. The key lies in trusting the process, maintaining patience, and being willing to engage in deep self-reflection.

The tools in The Call to Greatness Framework may initially feel like spinning your wheels. But for those who keep offering the invitation, who hold steady and continue to apply the framework, a breakthrough is often just moments away.

This is the potential of what The Call to Greatness Framework enables.

Why Using This Framework Is for Everyone, Not Just Leaders

If the potential to reverse the top challenges leaders are facing isn't enough, take a moment to think about these added benefits of consistently using The Call to Greatness Framework.

The biggest payoff of this framework lies in its consistency and reliability. It's a proven path to "how you could," regardless of circumstances. Your team learns to trust not just you but the framework itself. They come to understand that every conversation, no matter how challenging the starting point, will lead to actionable insight and personal growth.

People enter your leadership space tangled in drama and beliefs of "why they can't," and through each step of the framework, they shed layers of confusion that fuels unhelpful action. By the time they reach the final step, they're ready to move forward with confidence and empowerment to impact the situation.

This consistent approach is predictable for your team and reduces anxiety because your approach, supported by the framework, becomes a safe place for their challenges to land. With the framework as your anchor, you don't have to know all the answers of how to fix the issue; you can simply trust the steps and tools to reveal next right action for all involved.

Your task as a leader is to simply walk people through the framework. This positions you in the role of thought partner rather than authority figure. Trust deepens within your team because everyone faces the same invitation to greatness through these consistent steps. They now have shared language. This allows teammates to communicate and bring up tougher topics with neutral language, such as "In the spirit of cleaning up thinking . . ." or "In the spirit of finding our part and knowing our role . . ."

What's even more powerful is how The Call to Greatness Framework begins to live within your team's mindset, operating like an internal navigation system. Your leadership scales naturally because the framework's power isn't confined to your physical presence. These tools become part of how your team thinks, communicates, and operates.

The framework's exponential potential lies in its ability to replicate across your team and organization. As people experience its power, they naturally begin internalizing its steps, using them independently, and sharing them with others. Your leadership multiplies without your direct presence, as the tools become part of how your team takes issues head-on. This framework and the tools embedded within it cut through any victim-minded thinking, and the framework eventually becomes peer reinforced instead of leader led because colleagues can issue the call to greatness to each other in the moment, even without a leader present.

Your team learns to trust the cadence at which you will solve problems alongside them. The approach is predictable, consistent, and, for lack of a better term, soothing, because no matter what the problem may be, your team can rest assured that the issue will have a safe space to be addressed intentionally. The feelings or experience they are having will be validated, and you will hold space for them.

You won't lower the standard of excellence you know they are capable of; you'll up the support by walking them through the tools of The Call to Greatness Framework at the appropriate time. With your open heart and open mind, you'll support them in finding a place for impact in the situation. You'll reassure your team that you will stay with them as long as they need until they can see at least one possibility of next right action. Your steady approach builds trust, as they know their teammates will be called up just the same. This is actual empathy, and it is what people long for in the modern workplace.

People don't just learn to solve problems; they learn to lead themselves, support their teammates, and call their colleagues up to greatness. As the act of calling people up takes hold, every challenge becomes a chance at growth rather than a cause for complaint.

Now, if you're reading this as an individual contributor and are not yet a formal leader, the same framework is powerful because it's a way to find clarity and immediately know where to add value in any situation throughout your career. It is a simple approach that ensures that at every single moment, you're showing up as a low-drama, agile, flexible, and high-value contributor on your team. This is an increasingly important skill set in a world where jobs are consistently changing because of rapid disruption and shifting business needs.

Now, It's Your Turn . . . Are You In?

Looking back at the "I can see it" experience with the leaders in New York City, it occurred to me that all the alarming leadership trends being shared in the industry were present in that situation.

Several team members were completely disengaged and had not bought in to the organization's initiative. There was resistance to change, and there were managers ill-equipped to address it or coach through it. Most important, these managers couldn't focus on their bigger initiatives because their teams lacked the willingness to adopt the smaller ones already in place.

Then, with one five-minute tool and an invitation through The Call to Greatness Framework, the team moved through it. They went from a mindset of "why we can't" to "how we could." This all happened not because of me but because of the framework, which shows that anyone could have done it in that moment. This means that **moving forward, you can do it as well**.

I often ask people, "What leader impacted you the most in your career?"

Not a single response has been a story of someone who colluded, sympathized, and left them believing they were at the mercy of their circumstances.

What I mostly hear is a story about a leader who had the courage to lovingly and empathetically validate the challenge they were facing.

However, those leaders didn't just stop there. They proceeded to call them up to greatness, to take next right action, and to move forward anyway, even when it was hard.

Imagine being that leader for your team. That's what this book offers. Just as the team at the beginning of this book discovered in their trip through the call to greatness, next right action to succeed, in spite of the circumstances, is one round through The Call to Greatness Framework away.

I invite you to start issuing that call to your team. Let's get started.

DIGITAL TOOLKIT

Before you learn more about The Call to Greatness Framework and transforming how you lead your teams, let's make sure you are equipped with your toolkit and starter resources. Follow the QR code below to download The Call to Greatness Framework Toolkit PDF. Keep this on your desktop, on your phone, and printed close by to refer to often as you go through the day and support team members who are stuck. This toolkit contains a template of each tool as well as a tutorial video for each step of the framework to share with the person you are coaching.

PART I

LOVE PEOPLE UP

Tools Without Relationship Equals Rebellion

If you have picked up this book, you most likely have people you work with whom you hope to influence in a helpful way through your leadership. If your team happens to be falling short of their potential now, you're looking to unlock it. If they are currently delivering great results, you are hoping to continue fueling your team's development, growth, and evolution.

Whether either of these fits your situation or your team lands somewhere in between, this book shows you how to unlock that inherent greatness each person on your team possesses and, most important, how to encourage them to turn that spark of greatness into helpful action.

Seeing the jolt of energy, clarity, and positive action in someone you are influencing in this way is among the most meaningful parts of leadership. Supporting a team member as they shift from being stuck to unstuck, from helpless to empowered, from resistance to openness—the adrenaline buzz of one of these experiences can fuel the spirit of a leader for years.

This book gives you the powerful framework and tools to do this daily.

But with great power comes great responsibility.

A coach of mine once said, "Rules without relationship leads to rebellion. Alex, connection before correction." That moment has stayed with me for years. Without a foundation of love, relationship, and connection, there is no chance for real leadership or behavior change to happen.

The tools embedded in The Call to Greatness Framework have the power to unlock capabilities in your team that you've never seen before. But to ensure that those tools work as intended, we need to clarify your responsibility so that using them doesn't fall flat or backfire. As a leader, you have two core responsibilities each day to your team:

1. Love people up.
2. Call people up to be the best version of themselves.

Loving people up, in a broad sense, involves sharing appreciation for everyone on your team for bringing their unique gifts to your organization. It means acknowledging that they've chosen to bring those talents and efforts to support your organization's goals, mission, and vision. It calls for building a foundational relationship with each team member and understanding their personal goals, dreams, and career ambitions. It includes appreciating specific things they've done in the recent days, weeks, or months to go above and beyond for your clients, customers, patients, or colleagues. It is showing that, as a leader, you appreciate what makes them special and an integral asset to your team and the organization's culture.

In a more specific sense (and how it is most often referred to in this book), loving someone up means that when someone approaches you in need of leadership, you validate the experience they are having and the feelings associated with it. It is acknowledging the unpreferred reality they are sharing with you and holding space as they feel the feelings it is creating.

Calling people up means consistently connecting teams to their deeper purpose within the organization and inviting them to grow beyond perceived limitations as professionals. It's the intentional reminder of the meaningful contribution their work makes to the *worldplace* while lovingly challenging them to become their best selves in the *workplace*.

Leaders don't get permission to call someone up to greatness with the tools in this book if they haven't loved that individual up first.

In this book, you'll learn about several of these powerful tools that have the potential to call people up to greatness in challenging moments. Upon reading, your temptation may be to run off to that nagging leadership issue you've been chewing on and throw a tool at the situation. The attempt may leave your team perplexed, or land flat, or even make things worse. This unfortunately common occurrence in leadership is a textbook example of trying to call people up before loving them up first.

I remember a leadership group I was speaking to that had absorbed a sudden change in strategy that had caused some disruption. It seemed as if it was a complete 180-degree turn in what they were being asked to execute without being consulted. Believing I had built a good foundation of trust and rapport in the first couple of hours of our session, I quickly started a tool for the group to start solving problems and identifying risks so they could move forward, given what the organization now needed. As I asked the group to jump in and share more about their concerns, I noticed several arms had crossed in the audience, the temperature seemed to rise a bit, and I was now looking at a few faces with the metaphorical stink eye. I realized I had jumped too quickly into calling this group up to greatness without adequately loving them up. In other words, I hadn't taken a moment to validate the experience and feelings associated with their frustration of spending six months on a project only to have it pivoted in another direction with little notice.

This same problem comes up when a newly inspired leader, now equipped with a few tools from this book after attending a session, ambitiously sets out to use what they've learned to attempt to manipulate people to get what they want, or to finally get their team to *get it*. They apply the new technique, expecting a sudden shift and the seas to part for the person in front of them, and instead, the room fills with silence and awkwardness.

Each of these was an example of a leader forgetting to validate the experience or feelings of those involved and rushing into the call to greatness. It's the use of our tools without relationship, and the result was rebellion. They tried to call people up prior to first loving them up.

In fact, these situations (while more the exception and not the norm for leaders using our ideas with their teams) revealed something I had simply overlooked and whose importance I had misjudged. Leaders who unsuccessfully attempted to use the tools without this foundation were basically doomed from the start. More important, I had assumed that the way to practically love someone up and set the stage for the tools to perform their magic came naturally and easily for leaders. It dawned on me that this wasn't always the case.

The culmination of these insights is what clarified the first step of the Call to Greatness Framework and why it is so important.

CHAPTER 1

CALL TO GREATNESS STEP 1. VALIDATE THE EXPERIENCE OR FEELINGS

While there is no way to guarantee that you'll never mistime a call to greatness or skip too quickly past loving people up, there are some ways to ensure that you consistently strike the correct balance. This chapter explores the nuanced art of how to do this—acknowledging others' experiences and feelings about a challenge while maintaining an eye toward accountability and how they can succeed given the circumstances.

When coworkers face challenging work situations, the way leaders respond can empower growth, enable stagnation, or, in the worst cases, revert people backward in their development journey. The first step required to a successful call to greatness is **validating someone's experience or feelings about the challenge being faced**. And to do so requires a deeper understanding of the nuances of sympathy and empathy.

The Hidden Cost of Misguided Connection

With today's emphasis on emotional intelligence and psychological safety, leaders have embraced the call for greater empathy in the workplace (and rightly so). Yet in this noble and necessary pursuit, a concerning pattern has started to emerge: a confusion between empathy and sympathy. Understanding this distinction can not only make or break your effectiveness as a leader, but it is also a critical gauge as to whether you're fulfilling your leadership role at all.

This is important because in leadership, nobody comes to you for sympathy; what they crave is empathy. Getting comfortable at validating the experience or feelings of those you lead without collusion is directly connected to whether your leadership is truly based in empathy instead of sympathy.

Empathy allows you to validate someone's experience while fostering accountability and agency for the choices that could improve the situation. Sympathy starts on a similar path of validating someone's experience and feelings but leaves the person struggling, believing they are the innocent victim and at the mercy of their circumstances.

A story shared with me years ago helped me to fully *feel* the difference of what it is like to be "supported" by sympathy instead of empathy.

Imagine for a moment that you were experiencing crushing chest pains. You rush to the nearest emergency department, and the doctor asks, "You're having crushing chest pains? Does it feel like an elephant is sitting on your chest?"

Gasping for breath, you respond, "Yes! Exactly that!"

The medical provider's response? "Dang, me too."

You are now feeling a little uncomfortable and confused, when out comes another question from the provider: "Does the pain shoot down your left arm or your right arm?"

"My left arm!" you exclaim, pointing at it frantically.

Their response: "Oh wow, me too."

What is the point of this slightly ridiculous scene? You came into that emergency department for medical care, and you're starting to realize you aren't getting any.

What if your team is coming to you for leadership, and they are starting to realize they aren't getting any? In this case, your approach to helping them when they are stuck is to sympathize and leave them believing you are just as lost for a path forward as they are. Leaders should think about their leadership interactions with similar discipline.

Just as you'd expect a doctor to systematically assess and address your condition, your team needs you to help them navigate their challenges in the same way—through an intentional process.

In these situations, you need to ask yourself, *What is a consistent structure of thinking through an issue that will help this person in front of me to find the next helpful action?* Doing so allows leaders to show that they understand their people's challenges and feelings while still holding high standards and fostering personal accountability. Sympathy often lowers the standards and blames circumstances. Empathy holds the standard while upping the support and coaching. That increased support is what is experienced when someone goes through each reflection tool of The Call to Greatness Framework.

The Fork in the Road: Choosing Empathy over Sympathy

One of the biggest challenges with navigating the fine line of leading with empathy over sympathy is that in the real moments when your leadership is needed, both approaches begin with the same words: "I see you struggling." It's what happens next that determines whether a leader elevates into real leadership or diminishes the potential growth of the person in front of them.

When sympathy is the path chosen, the leader proceeds to agree with the person who is struggling, often colluding with them that they are the innocent victim and that they have no way to impact the circumstances. The person with the challenge is enabled to remain in a victim mindset with no consideration of a path to next right action given the challenge they've been presented with. When leaders confuse sympathy for empathy, they become coconspirators in their team's limited beliefs rather than architects of their transformation. The difference is whether you feed the victim-minded sense they are making of the situation or fuel their belief that they can succeed in spite of the circumstances.

Leaders who sympathize often run off to try to change or perfect the workplace reality instead of evolving people to be more skillful in their current reality. They tend to overmanage and underlead. They jump in to fix the situation instead of growing the capabilities of the employee who is stuck. This is justified by saying, "It's just faster for me to do it." This approach culminates in a cycle of codependency, leaving employees disempowered and unable to step fully into their roles. This zaps the motivation of employees and tempts leaders to play the underappreciated martyr who does their own job and everyone else's as well. Ultimately, leaders end up resenting their teams, and employees become less capable in their roles and stunted in their growth and evolution.

Sympathy does create connection and bonding, but not in a way that is healthy, helpful, or productive long-term. This is what makes it so enticing for leaders to sympathize, despite the destruction and havoc it causes.

The trap of sympathy often manifests as follows:

- Agreeing with all grievances
- Reinforcing learned helplessness
- Building connection through shared victimhood
- Lowering standards to match perceived limitations to achieving goals
- Decrease in problem-solving capability
- Increase in leadership codependency

Empathy chooses a different path altogether. It acknowledges the challenging reality while maintaining possibility. It validates feelings while inviting agency and the power of one's choices. It doesn't lower the standards but instead increases support and coaching around the challenge. Or, as you will soon learn, it validates the experience and feelings someone is having and eventually invites them to grow beyond the circumstances that are holding them back.

Guiding your team through the entire process of The Call to Greatness Framework isn't *just* about following steps; it's what transforms surface-level sympathy into genuine empathy. When leaders shy away from issuing this call, they leave their people sinking in the quicksand of sympathy while holding the rope of empathy just out of reach.

However, there's a colossal difference between being processed through a challenging situation and having a partner who facilitates you through it. **When leaders skip the human work and jump straight to the framework, even the most effective leadership approach in the world, applied without authentic connection, can become a form of elegant manipulation.** Your team can feel the difference.

The Keys to Validating the Experience

The first step in The Call to Greatness Framework, of validating someone's experience or feelings, is for you, as a leader, to embody and express this: "I see you, I hear you, *and* I acknowledge that this is a challenging situation for you."

This does not mean, however, that you also validate the perception of the situation—especially if the interpretations are causing those involved to suffer, wallow, or remain stuck.

This is important because validating someone's experience is not about agreeing that their circumstances are insurmountable or confirming their story that is fueling their helpless stance. This is validating the drama, not the feelings or experience, which only keeps people stuck—sympathy, in its purest form.

True validation achieved with empathy means acknowledging that yes, you're having feelings about the situation, but there are several positive possible choices available to you—not sometime in the future but right now.

For example, instead of replying with, "You're right, it's unacceptable they changed the policy without consulting you," a more fitting validation would be, "Yes, that is an unpreferred reality that the policy changed without our input, and I see you have some strong feelings about that. Given this and the new parameters, what ideas do you have to navigate your top three concerns that might hinder the success of the policy?"

The key is to acknowledge the emotion and the feelings without adding drama or reinforcing a victim mindset and lack of accountability. Great leaders can help people process emotions without getting bogged down in them. The goal isn't to eliminate feelings; it's to navigate through them in a more intentional way. Remember, your job as a leader is not to be your team's therapist. Your job is to act as that initial soft place to absorb the frustration and then to help point to the choices available to help in any given reality.

Building on this, here are ways to narrow in on what validating the experience actually means:

1. Recognizing the team members' feelings *without* suggesting those feelings should drive their behaviors or actions
2. Acknowledging the understandable nature of their reaction *without* reinforcing that it's the only possible response
3. Embracing the reality of the situation (no matter how unpreferred) *without* adding judgment, assumptions, or assignments of motive
4. Holding space to feel their feelings *without* justification, blame, or finger-pointing

Getting skillful at maintaining these distinctions allows you to create safety without collusion, to acknowledge a challenging reality without endorsing victim-minded thinking, and to love people up while creating the fertile ground necessary to call them up.

A leader's aim shouldn't be to keep people feeling safe and comfortable where they are currently stuck; it's to create a space safe enough to offer the invitation down the path of growing beyond it. When leaders validate someone's experience effectively and consistently, they reinforce an implicit promise that "I see you, *and* I believe in your capability to evolve." The *and* is essential—it's what separates the true validation of their issue from spiraling down the slippery slope of sympathy.

Let's look at a few more helpful examples of validating the experience or feelings.

Overwhelmed with workload

"I can see how much you're managing right now with a few team members on leave. That's a lot on your plate, and I can see why you're upset."

Dealing with a difficult coworker

"It can be challenging working with someone whose style is different from yours. I hear your frustration."

Passed over for a promotion

"Missing out on that opportunity you wanted—that's disappointing. I can see why you're hurt."

Navigating organizational change

"Major organizational changes like this can feel destabilizing. It makes sense that you're feeling uncertain and fearful."

Lack of resources

"Yes, these constraints are real. I hear how frustrated you are about working with limited resources."

Unclear expectations

"It's challenging when expectations feel unclear. I understand why that's infuriating for someone who cares about doing good work."

Below are a few more response **phrases to validate** *without* **colluding:**

- "I can see why this feels challenging."
- "That sounds incredibly frustrating, and I can see why you're upset."
- "Your reaction makes sense, given the situation."
- "I recognize this is a tough situation you're navigating."
- "I understand you're going through a difficult time, and that's perfectly valid."

In contrast, here are some **phrases that sympathize and enable victimhood:**

- "You're right: This stuff always happens to our team."
- "That's terrible. You definitely deserve better."
- "I can't believe they would treat you like this."
- "Nobody should have to deal with something like this."
- "Seriously? I can't believe we're back to this again."

While these are some starters to help you find your own go-to lines for common issues you are asked to help with, it is impossible to give examples for all situations. What is more helpful is to touch on some of the common pitfalls that come up when trying to successfully master validating someone's experience.

Common Pitfalls When Validating the Experience

Beyond the issue of prematurely rushing into using a tool to address a matter and skipping the step of validating the experience, there are a few additional pitfalls that will sabotage your chances of shifting into the call to greatness.

The Agreement Trap: It can be tempting to validate the experience by agreeing with the stories, interpretations, and sense the person is making of the experience. Validate the feelings or experience while resisting the urge to commiserate. If you find yourself agreeing with all negative assessments of the situation, that's a red flag.

The Fixing Reflex: Many leaders came up the ranks as doers who were promoted to leadership for getting things done. When someone comes to them with an issue, they fall back on old habits and jump in to fix it. Every time you rush in to fix a situation, you rob someone of their chance to evolve. The irony of this fixing reflex and heroic leadership is that it creates helpless teams. Suspend the inclination to jump in and fix things.

The Story Expansion: Avoid adding to their narrative with your own similar experiences or grievances. This can amplify the drama and reinforce the belief of "why they can't."

The Dreaded One-Upper: "Oh, you think that's bad! Let me tell you a story about what happened to me years ago." To connect and help the person feel better, avoid delving into an experience you've had that was just a little tougher, more annoying, or insurmountable. This tends to backfire and negate the experience they're having.

The Reflection Ruiner: Many leaders struggle when there is silence, treating it as the problem instead of the necessary starting point to insight. That space of processing can be uncomfortable, yet sometimes giving it a few moments longer can be all the difference in adequately validating the experience and opening readiness to start moving beyond the issue.

The Overvalidation Loop: Watch for signs that validation is becoming a comfort zone and a way to emotionally blackmail you into delaying necessary growth or action the person can take to grow beyond their challenging circumstances.

When Is Enough Validation Enough?

It is important to realize that validation isn't the destination; it is the launchpad. It's critical, but the real magic happens once you've gotten past it.

With that in mind, how do you know when it's time to move on to calling someone up? When have you adequately validated someone's experience about the issue? Or put simply, when is enough validation enough?

A leader once interrupted me midsession and jokingly asked,

"Alex, can we just settle this? Is it thirty-eight seconds of validating and listening to feelings? Two minutes and seventeen seconds? Five minutes and forty-nine seconds? I need the exact threshold where I'm allowed to move past feelings and start solving."

The length of time for proper validation isn't something exact I can give you. It takes discernment. It's about feel. It's situational. My short response is simply to connect as a human to the other human(s) entangled in the issue and trust your read on it. If your heart and mind are open and you sense you're connected to those involved, you're most likely close to the bullseye. Trust yourself.

The length of validation isn't about scripting perfection; it's about authenticity. One genuine sentence, a reassuring breath with eye contact, or a connected moment of silence that acknowledges reality while not closing out possibilities for "how we could" is worth more than an hour of commiserating. When you really understand the human condition and your team members' challenges, you can validate quickly without adding drama to the situation.

As your team begins to trust your approach as a leader, most situations only require a touch-and-go interaction in which we meaningfully acknowledge the experience and emotions, then shift naturally into focus on "how we could."

However, some situations demand a longer layover. Many professions I speak to have leaders who support teams that deal with deeply challenging experiences, sometimes on the daily. A healthcare leader once voiced concern during a session by asking, "How could I possibly use this framework when my nurse has just lost a patient, or when a colleague of mine has just watched a family crumble under a devastating diagnosis? I just can't see me saying, basically, 'Dang, I see why you are struggling. Now, given that, what would be next right action?'"

This gets to the heart of leadership discernment. In moments of deep human suffering—the death of a patient, a devastating personal loss, a traumatic workplace event—it should go without saying that validation isn't just a touch-and-go; it's a full stop. Holding space and simply being present become the entire point of the interaction. No clever transitions, no shifts toward problem-solving—just pure presence and deep validation.

The key is recognizing that this framework, like any leadership approach, operates on a spectrum. Most workplace challenges—project setbacks, interpersonal conflicts, process frustrations—are sufficiently addressed with the touch-and-go approach. But we can't let the existence of rare profound moments invalidate a framework that serves us well in most daily leadership interactions and many high-impact situations.

While having an alarm clock go off to let you know when the person is ready to start growing beyond the challenge would be ideal, this is simply not something that will be invented anytime soon. There are, however, some cues and readiness signals to keep in mind that someone has most likely felt sufficiently validated and is ready for the invitation to be called up to greatness:

- Their breathing becomes more regulated.
- Watch for emotional regulation—has the person started to compose themselves or returned closer to neutral in their demeanor? Has the charge around the situation simmered down a bit? For example, Marcus bursts into his supervisor Elena's office, furious about a difficult client meeting: "They completely blindsided me with new demands! I felt so unprepared and embarrassed!" Elena validates the feelings by saying, "That sounds really frustrating. Being surprised in a client meeting is tough." Marcus continues sharing additional annoyances as Elena listens intently and holds slightly more space for the validation of his experience. Throughout the additional few minutes, Marcus's pacing slows, he takes a seat, he takes a sip of a water that Elena had grabbed

from her stash, and his expression shifts from anger to contemplation. These are all good signs of emotional regulation taking place with support from a leader.

- Notice shifts in their language.
  - You notice less extreme language and fewer phrases like "this *always* happens" or "they *never* support us."
  - What's being shared has shifted from emotional to analytical.
  - You're hearing more "I" statements instead of "they" or "them."
  - You observe a problem-solving orientation (i.e., is there an opening for "what can we start doing about it?").
  - Pay attention to future-focused questions or ideas (ideas about the future are often in the spirit of how we could move forward, while ideas about the past are often about blame, finger-pointing, resentments, and grudges).
- Their tone of voice has softened, or their posture has become more open.
- You can sense some curiosity to move beyond the stuck-ness.

While these can all be good indicators, it's important to keep in mind that someone may never feel they're fully ready for a call to greatness, because the self-reflection involved often creates moments of discomfort. While you do have an enormous responsibility of trying to meet people where they are, waiting for someone to be "ready" for evolving beyond their limiting beliefs is often enabling their resistance to reality. The reality is that they're capable right now, even if they don't feel ready. They have been put in this situation, at this time, for a reason, and your role is to remind them that this is the very place they can add value.

While every frustration your team encounters may not need intervention, every frustration *does* have a call to greatness embedded in it. You'll miss some opportunities, let your team down from time to time, and screw this up, but only daily. I know I have as a leader.

Great leadership isn't about applying these steps and tools rigidly; it's about reading the humanness of the moment accurately and responding appropriately. A general rule of thumb is that people often won't engage with your solutions until they feel fully seen in their struggle. If you find yourself in doubt about whether to start the call to greatness, err on the side of more love. The path to "how we could" will still be there when you sense the time is right.

In saying that, choosing "more love" in Reality-Based Leadership means loving people enough to reveal their own empowerment so they can step into the power they *already* have to succeed anyway. It means believing in their capability so deeply that you refuse to reinforce their self-limiting beliefs about "why they can't." Sometimes the most loving act is affirming their struggle *and* their agency: "I know this is hard *and* I know you can handle it" in the same breath.

The most profound way to validate someone's experience isn't to agree with their interpretation of the situation (especially if it is causing suffering); it's to believe so deeply in their capacity to transcend it that they begin to believe it too. The good news is that you don't have to be a spiritual guru or seasoned leader to make this happen. You need simply to learn how to apply the tools baked into The Call to Greatness Framework, and this belief naturally happens with those you lead.

Your team's pain at work deserves acknowledgment, but their potential demands action. The uncomfortable truth is that validation without a call to greatness is just sophisticated stagnation. There's a sacred moment when feeling heard transforms into feeling capable—when "I see you" becomes "I see what's possible for you."

They've been seen. They've been heard. Now's the time to cross the bridge to what's possible.

THE FULL CALL TO GREATNESS IN ACTION—VIRAL ON TIKTOK

I couldn't believe what the team was telling me.

A decade's worth of work had just come to fruition.

We had just gone viral on TikTok. The first video was skyrocketing into the millions of views, and the second video was sprinting close behind, approaching a million as well. We had officially broken through with our recent marketing efforts, and this was going to transform our business!

Walking into the meeting with our founder the next day (or should I say floating into the meeting), prepared to be lauded and thanked, I was shocked when the tone of the meeting took an abrupt turn.

Our founder began, "I've called this emergency meeting because I want to revisit our social strategy, especially on the platform TikTok, due to some of the comments on the videos. I have some concern with how they might negatively impact our brand."

I couldn't even suppress my perplexity. I felt a confusion so big that I was using face muscles I'd never had. My mind reeled and my blood boiled as I sat in that meeting, trying to hold it together.

By some spark of chance or divine intervention, our founder was pulled out for an urgent client call before proceeding with the meeting. Completely rattled, I faded to my desk area to gather myself. With stressful thoughts flooding my mind, a pain in my neck, and my stomach doing circles, it became obvious to me that I was in an unpreferred reality. It was an open invitation to a trip through The Call to Greatness Framework—but only if I was interested in next right action when I returned to the meeting.

continued

These next ten minutes would be crucial for how I spoke up, showed up, or took action in the meeting after our founder finished her call.

I started with Step 1 of The Call to Greatness Framework, taking a moment to feel my feelings and validate my experience. I sat with it a bit, acknowledging that I was really surprised and frustrated about the unexpected announcement and shift in strategy. Still holding hope of arriving at the next best action to contribute to the meeting, I knew it was time to move into Step 2 of The Call to Greatness Framework, cleaning up my thinking.

PART II

CALL PEOPLE UP

While loving people up establishes a necessary foundation of safety, calling people up is the invitation to possibility. You have validated their experience and cracked open the window to start leading them toward growth. Now is the time to call them up to greatness and begin tilting the energy toward "how they could."

At its broadest, calling people up means reconnecting people to the deeper purpose of their work and how it connects directly to the important mission of the organization they've chosen to work for. This is a sacred link that is often lost in the daily grind. More specifically, in calling people up, leaders accept the responsibility of refusing to leave people stuck in their belief that their current circumstances are insurmountable. It is the intentional act of helping people move beyond their perceived limitations about their challenges, not by fixing their issues but by walking alongside them as they discover their own ability to impact them.

This is the moment when leadership actually happens. It is the delicate space between supporting someone as they process a challenging situation and illuminating a new path so they can evolve beyond it.

Continuing The Call to Greatness Framework: From Validation to Action

It's best to imagine calling people up as a transformational journey. Each person enters your leadership space carrying their challenges and, through an intentional progression of reflection, emerges with clarity on how to move forward. When executed with skill and heart, progression embedded in the framework transforms scattered venting and frustration into helpful next steps, regardless of the depth of the challenge. Within one focused conversation, those you lead leave with clear direction and renewed empowerment.

The Secret Sauce Is in the Sequence

While you may gravitate to certain favorite tools in this book, these steps must be followed in order. Just like a combination lock, the real breakthrough happens when each number is turned in sequence. We've already explored Step 1—validating the experience or feelings. From there, The Call to Greatness Framework continues through four additional and distinct steps:

1. Clean up thinking (about the issue).
2. Find your part (in the situation).
3. Know your role (in the solution).
4. Take next right action.

Each step builds on the previous one, creating deeper clarity as to how team members can best impact the situation. This isn't about rushing anyone to action; it's intentional transformation.

In saying that, more experienced practitioners of the framework share that next right action can become clear before completing all steps. While you can certainly move forward when the path ahead is obvious, don't mistake early clarity for optimal clarity. The framework isn't simply about finding an answer to move forward; it's about finding the best answers for next right action.

Be mindful not to engage in what I call skimming the growth opportunity or intellectualizing the framework. This is where, in the name of efficiency, you move people past the steps without completing the full process of the reflective tool. Rushing past steps is like scanning chapter headings without reading the book. By getting just the gist of what's happening, you miss the gold. Doing so often masks the best next right actions and, in the worst cases, leads to next wrong action instead.

Now that you understand the importance of following the sequence, let's dive deep into Step 2: Cleaning Up Thinking.

This is where the real transformation begins to take shape.

CHAPTER 2

CALL TO GREATNESS STEP 2. CLEAN UP THINKING: THE EDIT YOUR STORY TOOL

My wife, two-year-old son, and I were at the Dallas airport, waiting to board a flight to attend a childhood friend of mine's wedding. We were checked in and ready to fly when my son asked to ride my suitcase on the way to our gate. Cool, confident dad that I am, I sidestepped my wife's "Be careful" and helped my little man mount up. Off we went.

As we made our way to the gate, only a few minutes' walk away, fellow travelers commented on the cuteness. Then, in the split second of a side glance, our little guy suddenly catapulted face first onto the floor. Chaos quickly ensued. Guilt kicked in immediately.

Grabbing an extra shirt from my backpack, we did what we could to contain the bleeding and headed to the nearest emergency department. My mind raced with frightening possibilities: Had I seen all his front teeth? Were his gums and nose damaged? Would surgery be required? How bad would this be? I kept thinking, *His face is going to be changed forever because of me!*

At the ER, the provider calmly said, "Let's clear the wound and see what we are working with." As they worked (not fast enough for my liking), their slow, steady approach gave my panic time to climb a few peaks. I wanted them to do *something now* to make it better! When my son's face had been properly cleaned, the assessment began. I could see teeth but also a large cut on his upper lip. Major surgery would be required! I knew it!

After a quick huddle, the care provider team approached and told me, "He is going to be just fine." All his teeth were intact, there was no facial damage found, and cuts on the lip typically heal with minimal issues 99.9 percent of the time (which they did).

The lessons of that experience stayed with me: Before jumping to what you think might be next right action (surgery), first clean up thinking and get a clear view of the problem (teeth intact, minor cut that will heal).

If I had done that, I wouldn't have suffered the pain of my son's massive, life-altering facial surgery, which never happened. All he needed was a pacifier and a few weeks of his body's natural healing process.

My story is a metaphor for the way that modern leaders can benefit from cleaning up thinking when call to greatness opportunities emerge. Until you have cleaned up your team's thinking about the problem, taking action to solve it will be unhelpful.

Too often, problems springing from an unpreferred reality appear bigger than they are. Without clean thinking, people often move into an unhelpful cycle of ruminating about the unpreferred reality—or worse, pulling in coworkers to vent or complaining or blaming other people or the circumstances instead of working to overcome the issue. At the root of all these common responses is the ego.

At Reality-Based Leadership, we uncovered in our research over the last two decades that ego-based behaviors are the number one source of workplace drama. Ego is that endless chatter going on in your head throughout the day that narrates your world. Listen closely, and you'll notice ego is the judger of all things and the creator of all stories. These stories and judgments tend to skew negative in nature. Left uninvestigated, ego-based thinking fuels judging, gossiping, tattling, scorekeeping, ruminating, comparing, and ultimately helplessness. Unfortunately, you can't simply get rid of ego; it is part of human nature.

Ego is often confused with confidence. Confidence is based on the conviction that you have great information, skills, and expertise that you can add to the collective input of your team in a helpful way. It is anchored in the belief that together, we are genius. By contrast, ego is "*I know* the way, and I am the smartest one in the room to get us there."

Ego has a small portion to play in fueling the confidence that enables you to step into the unique skills you bring to your job, but the bigger chunk of ego is not so helpful.

In the workplace, the ego more typically steps proudly into one job: It takes what happens in your reality and distorts the information in your favor—painting us as an innocent victim and everyone else as the villains. And it is relentless in fulfilling that job. Looking at the world through ego is like wearing prescription glasses all day but with the wrong prescription. Ego constantly scans your environment, fogging the facts and looking for insult, often where there isn't any. It prefers certainty over accuracy and would rather be dead wrong about a situation than experience the discomfort of uncertainty.

In fact, if ego can keep teams convinced that problems are too complex, work has too many competing priorities, and processes are riddled with too many moving parts and involve too many (possibly incompetent or uncooperative) people, drama and stress will take the stage. When teams are under the spell of the ego and the limiting stories it creates, next right action is elusive or, in the worst of cases, leads to behaviors that contribute to next wrong or unhelpful action toward the situation.

For these reasons, the second step of The Call to Greatness Framework is to invite people to clean up thinking. This involves leaders inviting a reconsideration of the narrative that the ego is making of the situation at hand, because its additions to the situation are usually unhelpful, counterproductive to solutions, and detrimental to team dynamics.

The fundamental skill of cleaning up thinking is a significant first step to moving a team from frustration about a less-than-ideal situation to clarity and action toward the ideal future. Just like the health-care providers cleaned up the bloody mess of my son's injury before acting, teams should also clean up the often-foggy thinking initially offered up by the ego when a challenge emerges.

A Little Venting Never Hurt Anyone, Did It?

Self-reflection is key to defusing drama at work. It is the foundation for cleaning up thinking, dropping into personal accountability, and identifying next right action.

In leadership, the disruptive behavior of venting happens to be the ego's favorite mechanism for avoiding self-reflection and is often confused with the productive behavior of sharing a feeling. Of course, it's important to be supportive of people's feelings. It's essential to building relationships, instilling trust, creating psychological safety, and establishing healthy team dynamics. Sharing these feelings is core to being human. And it's also imperative that leaders help clarify the difference between sharing a feeling and venting.

Sharing a feeling takes only a sentence. The ego then tends to distort the sense being made about the situation by venting, which adds story to keep the feeling alive. Let's look at an example between Owen and his colleague Jordan.

Feeling

I'm upset at Jordan because he didn't get me the information I needed, and it made me late for my deadline.

Sense being made of the feeling (the story)

Jordan is trying to sabotage my career and does this crap on purpose. It is all about making me look bad in front of the higher-ups because he wants someone else to get that open position. He holds grudges, always talking about how he had to grind in his career to get to where he is and now wants the younger generation to suffer like he did. He's been totally out to get me since my kid threw a ball and hit his kid in the head at a basketball game seven years ago, just because I laughed and didn't apologize . . .

The critical point here is that feeling upset is valid, but the suffering is being caused by the added story. The reality is true (Owen doesn't have the information he needs, so he missed a deadline). However, the sense being made of why he missed the deadline has been skewed by the ego's story.

Without questioning the story the ego is adding, which caused the bulk of the frustration, Owen's venting fuels the stance of being the victim of Jordan's behavior. There is little chance of finding next right action to succeed when you're focused on venting. A "how we could" leader encourages a different approach.

Validating the experience and feelings is the first step: "I can see you're frustrated that you didn't get the information you needed to complete the report by the deadline. That's happened to me before, and I can see why you're upset."

But a leader who aims to truly support ends with a call to greatness by inviting people to reconsider the sense they're making of the experience. This offers them an opportunity to clean up thinking about the unpreferred reality.

You may have heard the aphorism that "the truth will set you free." I've found this always to be the case. For this reason, my favorite questions for people when they are venting are "Is it true?" and "What do you know for sure?"

Presented with these two questions, Owen was encouraged to write down his verbal venting on paper. Once that was done, he was asked to cross out anything he couldn't know *for sure*. Here is what it looked like:

> *I'm upset at Jordan because he didn't get me the information I needed, and it made me late for my deadline.* ~~He is trying to sabotage my career and does this crap on purpose. It is all about making me look bad in front of the higher-ups because he wants someone else to get that open position. He holds grudges, always talking about how he had to grind in his career to get to where he is. He wants everyone to suffer like he did. He's been totally out to get me since our kids got into that fight at the basketball game seven years ago because I laughed and didn't apologize . . .~~

Without changing anything, the simple step of self-reflection changed everything.

When looking at the cleaned-up story, a facepalm was in order from Owen, and his response was a lighthearted, "In the future, I suppose I could put a reminder on Jordan's calendar a few days before the deadline and give him a quick call the week before. This would all take me two minutes at the most. For now, I can grab a coffee with him and share my concerns directly."

By simply cleaning up the thinking about the situation, the obvious next right action emerged. For Owen, his ego was no longer clouding his thinking, and with the facts remaining, he had a clear path to achieving his goals of hitting deadlines and maintaining a great working relationship with his colleague. Once a person has stopped judging and cleaned up their thinking, the natural inclination is to start helping.

The key to success in this step of the call to greatness is making the "What do you know for sure?" self-reflection visual. This is easily accomplished by using your first leadership tool embedded in the framework, called **Edit Your Story**.

This tool supports people whose ego might be adding unhelpful fuel to the fire for the challenge at hand. The tool helps them dissolve what's not real to focus on the true source of the feelings that are keeping them stuck. It is a simple exercise for when people feel unclear, frustrated, angry, confused, annoyed, or helpless about the work in front of them. In just a few minutes, the tool can clarify the problem, reduce stress, reveal ways to improve the situation, and inspire next right action.

The purpose of this tool is to create a visual representation of the story, judgments, thoughts, and beliefs someone has about the challenge they are experiencing by transferring it from their heads to paper. Think of it as capturing the story they are about to share, word for word, about the situation that has them stuck. In short, they are documenting all unclean thinking in one space.

THE EDIT YOUR STORY TOOL

To begin, all that is needed is a pencil or pen and something to write on. This tool can be done as a group, with each person writing out their own story about the situation, or it can be done one-on-one with a colleague or leader guiding them through the steps. If preferred, the story can be typed in a computer document or email draft.

Here is how it works:

1. Ask the person to write down the story running through their head about the issue—every unfiltered thought and detail. And I mean everything! Don't hold them back. This can include the backstory, assignments of motive, details about those involved, judgments, theories, etc. Ultimately, they are capturing a written version of their verbal venting.
2. Ask the author to go through the written story, line by line, and ask themselves, *Is this true? Can I really know that it's true? Do I know this for sure? What are the facts?*
3. If something isn't 100 percent certain, they must cross it out. Words like "they always" and "he never" are red flags. Have them clarify the frequency of those behaviors. Have them double-check sentences that assign motives to others. If they can't remember exactly what was said, they must investigate it, clean it up, or toss it out. Hyperbole like "I've told her a million times" and "this is the thousandth time this has happened" must be clarified with factual numbers or eliminated. The goal isn't to change the story of the person but to simply allow the facts to remain.
4. Review the edited story. The truth or accuracy of the experience or problem (or as close as a person can get) now is revealed, and they have reduced the judgment and ditched the drama.

5. Acknowledge this revealed reality and ask, "Given what's left after you've edited your story, how could you help? What is next right action you can take, given this unpreferred reality?" We recommend creating at least three tangible action steps and encourage buy-in to move forward with them.

Digital Toolkit: Want to access the tutorial video and template to help you clean up thinking? Scan the QR code below to download the tool as well as the full digital Call to Greatness Framework Toolkit.

Understanding the First Burst of Initial Clarity and Action Ideas

The Edit Your Story tool experience is notorious for creating "duh" moments because it shows many obvious next steps to take once the ego has simmered down. But as mentioned earlier, be careful not to confuse initial clarity for optimal clarity when going through The Call to Greatness Framework.

You can no doubt forge ahead with the ideas you now have from completing this tool, and, in most cases, progress will happen. However, those action steps run the risk of your team still not knowing their part in what created the situation in the first place and what their role is supposed to be in the solution in the short and long term. In other words, these initial action steps you have from completing the first tool could address surface-level symptoms of the problems but not the deeper root cause. For this reason, I suggest documenting these ideas or keeping them top of mind for now and then let them continue to get refined or sharpened as you proceed through the remaining steps of the framework.

The athlete in me hears a coach's voice in my head saying, "You can get away with it for a while, but cutting corners eventually catches up to you."

That said, if the unpreferred reality seems to be minor, use your discernment. If your read on the situation is that it is a touch-and-go call to greatness moment and next right action ideas produced at this point suffice, run with them.

Now that you've got your first tool and you know how to use it, let's look at how this simple practice has solved many business problems in the real world.

THE FULL CALL TO GREATNESS IN ACTION—VIRAL ON TIKTOK

When our founder informed us that she wanted to halt our social media strategy despite our recent successes, my ego immediately took over and began to add its commentary to this brief (and surprising for me) announcement.

I thought, *This woman has lost her mind. She obviously doesn't understand marketing or how to run a business, especially in a viral moment. This is a once-in-a-lifetime breakthrough, a chance to finally transform the business to the next level, and she's ruining it. She's backing out of success and wasting a decade of progress that we've worked hard for. She's purposely sabotaging this breakthrough, and it'll never happen again.* I'm ashamed to admit that it crossed my mind that we should get her into a nursing home.

Once I had finished validating my feelings, I took a moment to scribble those initial thoughts on paper to set up the Edit Your Story tool. Once I applied the anchor of "What do I know for sure?" my paper looked like this:

> ~~This woman has lost her mind.~~ *I am in a meeting with our team about social media strategy.* ~~She obviously doesn't understand marketing or how to run a business, especially in a viral moment. She is blowing up that~~ *our videos going viral on TikTok have some negative comments being shared.* ~~This is a once-in-a-lifetime breakthrough, and it's a chance to catapult the business to the next level, and she's ruining it because~~ *she wants to adjust her strategy with the videos! She is wondering how this may impact the brand.* ~~She's backing out of success and wasting a decade of progress that we've worked hard for.~~ *I am so frustrated* ~~because she's purposely sabotaging this breakthrough, and it'll never happen again.~~

Pulling out the facts without my judgments, stories, and assignments of motives, here was what remained from the Edit Your Story tool:

- I am in a meeting with our team about social media strategy.
- We have videos going viral on TikTok with some negative comments being shared.
- Our founder is choosing to adjust her strategy with these videos.
- She is wondering about how this may impact the brand.
- I am now frustrated.

With the clean story, I simmered down a bit. But I was not yet clear on next right action when I returned to the meeting. It was time to continue to Step 3 and find my part in the situation.

Love Your Boss Again

During a coaching session, Pierson confided he was feeling overwhelmed, stressed out, and frustrated at work. Things were so bad with his manager that he was considering leaving his job. Pierson was in an unpreferred reality that so many people find themselves in. I asked him to tell me more:

> *Out of the blue, my boss called to check on a project, micromanaging. She is treating me like a child. Again. True, the project is behind schedule, but my boss should trust me and my team enough to know we'll get on top of things before we're scheduled to present an update to leadership.*
>
> *But that's not all. Our division has been asked to cut its budget, and I'm sure they are targeting certain groups. My boss is setting me up to fail because she's probably heard I am thinking about applying for a promotion. I'd be a great candidate, but I think she wants to promote one of her friends instead.*
>
> *I'm worried the project might be cancelled, which would be the third time in one year. If that happens, people are going to think I'm not contributing at work. What if I get fired? My daughter is in veterinary school, and she wants to help the pandas in East Asia. If I get fired, those pandas are going to die!*

Did you feel stressed reading Pierson's story? How many times have you had your own version of this story or heard a coworker tell you something similar? How many times have you heard someone complaining about their manager and sympathized, colluded, and left them believing they are at the mercy of their circumstances?

I heard the despair in Pierson's voice as well as the heightened stress that charged Pierson's words. I knew more venting about his problems wouldn't help. It was time to begin the Edit Your Story tool. First, I validated his feelings and experience: "I appreciate you sharing what's going on, and I can see you're struggling and why you are frustrated with your boss. I remember times when my boss and I weren't seeing eye-to-eye, and it was tough."

After a brief pause, I continued, "But if you're game, it might be helpful if we took a second look at the story you shared. Let's write out everything you just shared on this piece of paper, and we'll do a quick scan to see if we can know everything for sure. Let's Edit the Story and see if that helps at all.

Pierson agreed to the exercise. After five minutes or so, below is what the tool looked like on the paper in front of us:

> *Out of the blue, my boss called to check on a project,* ~~micromanaging. She is treating me like a child. Again.~~ *True, the project is behind schedule,* ~~but my boss should trust me and my team enough to know we'll get on top of things before~~ *we're scheduled to present an update to leadership on Thursday.*
>
> *But that's not all. Our division has been asked to cut its budget,* ~~and I'm sure they are targeting certain groups. My boss is setting me up to fail because she's probably heard~~ *I am thinking about applying for a promotion. I'd be a great candidate*~~, but I think she wants to promote one of her friends instead.~~
>
> *I'm worried the project might be cancelled, which would be the third time in one year.* ~~If that happens, people are going to think I'm not contributing at work. What if I get fired?~~ *My daughter is in veterinary school, and she wants to help the pandas in East Asia.* ~~If I get fired, those pandas are going to die!~~

Pulling out the facts that remained after the tool, this was the reality of the situation:

- Pierson's boss called to check on a project.

- His boss prefers to get more detail than he'd like to give. (This removed the "micromanager" judgment.)
- The project is behind.
- A project update to leadership is scheduled for Thursday.
- His division has been asked to cut its budget.
- He is thinking about applying for a promotion. He'd be a great candidate.
- Pierson is worried that the project might get cancelled.
- If this project is cancelled, it will be the third time in one year.
- His daughter is attending vet school and wants to help pandas in East Asia.

Pierson's unedited, ego-fueled story caused stress, anxiety, and overwhelm, which led to excuses, finger-pointing, and a sense of helplessness. Pierson had cast himself as a victim of a manipulative boss. His venting to colleagues at work (and even more to his family at home) offered a distorted view of the situation and perpetuated negative energy. Going through the tool helped Pierson clean up his story and clarify the facts.

I asked the final question of the Edit Your Story tool to turn the newfound clarity into initial next right action ideas: "Given this reality, what can you do to help?"

Pierson realized that his boss had just asked for a status update—as bosses everywhere do. And he was behind. The clean thinking led him to rearrange his work so that he and his team could focus, catch up, and be ready for the presentation. Because his boss preferred more detail than he traditionally liked to give, he arranged a meeting and asked, "Given my goal is to work together with less check-ins and your goal seems to be receiving a certain amount of detail, how might we meet in the middle?" With this clean thinking, next right action became obvious: to improve the relationship and trust with the boss and deliver the results she was looking for.

Nothing externally in the situation had changed for Pierson. Same boss, same deadlines, and same update requests. However, after completing the Edit Your Story tool, Pierson created a better working relationship with his boss, established clearer boundaries, and reinvigorated his energy at work. The same boss he once loathed was now one he understood and started getting great results with.

This often happens once we've questioned the sense being made of an unpreferred reality—and from that new clarity, we can take our next helpful right action. Pierson had dissolved what wasn't true and what was causing additional frustration, and that made all the difference. Pierson, in some ways, changed everything without changing anything.

Love Your Job Again

This tool also helped to clean up thinking about a less-than-ideal work reality facing members of a large sales team in the medical equipment industry I was consulting with. Several employees complained about feeling stressed and resentful because sales reps weren't completing all the information they needed on orders. One sales support agent I'll call Cara was particularly peeved. As part of the training, I'd asked the entire team to write down their stories. Cara agreed to share hers.

> *I have worked in sales support for eight years. Last week, I had yet another order come in with information missing. We've told [sales rep] Devon and his sales team a hundred times that we need all this information to get orders processed in a timely fashion.*
>
> *They are obviously lazy, and it's equally obvious the sales team doesn't value all that we do for them. They always say that they care about us, but this behavior never changes, so clearly, they don't.*

The salespeople know we are going to bail them out every single time they mess up. I'm always having to save the day around here by filling in all the gaps in information. They get to bring in the big-shot commissions, but they don't realize that this place would fall down without all that I do behind the scenes! They just don't appreciate all that we do.

After she'd shared her story, she agreed to take the next step of the Edit Your Story tool in front of the group. Typically, leaders in the company had said things such as, "That's just the way it is around here. Don't expect anything less. People (in sales) make the big bucks, so nobody holds them accountable to anything," which had added to the group's frustration and feelings of being victims.

I began by validating her feelings and experience with, "Dang, Cara, that is tough. I can see why it is so frustrating to have to pick up what people missed. I get frustrated when I am in situations like that." From there, I asked her to use her written-down story to reconsider the sense she was making of the experience because it was causing her suffering.

Asking her to scan each sentence, I invited her to consider the questions, "Is that true? Can you really know that it is true? What do you know for sure?" Her story after the self-reflection narrowed down to this:

- I have worked in sales support for eight years.
- My job is to support sales.
- I had an order with missing information.
- It was Devon's client.
- We've had meetings with sales reps about filling out information.

- The goal is to get the order processed quickly.
- Sales team members say they care about us.

After seeing her cleaned-up story, Cara said, "I guess if you look at it this way, the situation isn't nearly as frustrating." In reality, an order with missing information wasn't the source of her stress. Instead, it was the unquestioned story she was believing about the situation and her colleagues' motives.

We moved on to the final step of the Edit Your Story tool: "Given this reality and your role as sales support, what could you do to help? What step could you take to add value?"

Cara's answer came quickly: "I could pick up the phone, which my company provides for free, and reach out to the customer to confirm final details."

After the activity, one of Cara's colleagues also had a helpful realization. She said, "You mentioned this was one of your biggest annoyances in your job right now, correct? But imagine that your biggest wish was granted and that all salespeople from here on out would fill in all the information in the system. What would happen to your job?"

Cara had an epiphany: "Now that I think about it, sales would be spending less time selling and getting new clients. They'd be doing part of *my* job. Oh wait, maybe they wouldn't *need* sales support if that was happening. That might also mean that the organization wouldn't need *my* job."

Through the Edit Your Story tool, people often discover that most of what they are upset about *never even happened.* In other words, the bulk of the stress comes from the narrative they add on to the situation, not the situation itself. The tool helped Cara realize that a large chunk of her career had been spent being upset about *doing her daily job*—supporting sales—for which she received a paycheck and benefits. In this situation, nothing had changed physically for Cara except the ego-generated stories she had attached to the experiences alongside her colleagues. The sales reps no longer represented an obstacle and annoyance; they were the reason she *had* a job.

Cara revealed that if she'd had the Edit Your Story tool sooner, her stress, frustration, and annoyance might not have built up to the point she was so resentful about something she could easily remedy. Most important, her realization immediately improved her relationship with the sales team and her other colleagues. Helping, as opposed to judging, became her default, and love for her job trickled back in.

I Screw This Up, but Only Daily

True confession: I still get hooked by the unclean thinking fueled by ego, even after years of using this tool personally. One of the more recent examples happened during a massive travel week during one of the busiest times of year for me.

My schedule had me on your classic "rock-star" tour of Kohler, Wisconsin; Key West, Florida; Minneapolis, Minnesota; Memphis, Tennessee; and a final hop, skip, and a jump back home to Dallas, Texas. Adding to the week's excitement, I was to give speeches on the hallowed grounds of two of the most prestigious health-care organizations in the United States. It was a dream come true.

Riding the adrenaline of the week, I scurried out of a transformational session with the client in Key West with an hour to get to the airport. Looking ahead to Minneapolis with the first of those two prestigious clients, I threw my backpack and carry-on suitcase into the back of the rental car. As the hatch of the rental SUV closed, I whipped around to the driver's seat and pulled on the handle.

I pulled again.

And again.

And one more time with enough force to nearly separate my shoulder.

Panic and dread flooded my body. My first thought was, *Because I'm now going to obviously miss my flight, maybe I could drive all the way there* (although my keys were locked in the car!). I'm ashamed to admit the next frantic idea resulted in a scan of the parking lot to see which car might be a good one to take off with (only kidding!). Ego-induced grand theft auto would have been next wrong action as well.

Then came a breakthrough: "I can Uber there!" A quick search on my phone revealed what that journey would have looked like (see figure 2.1).

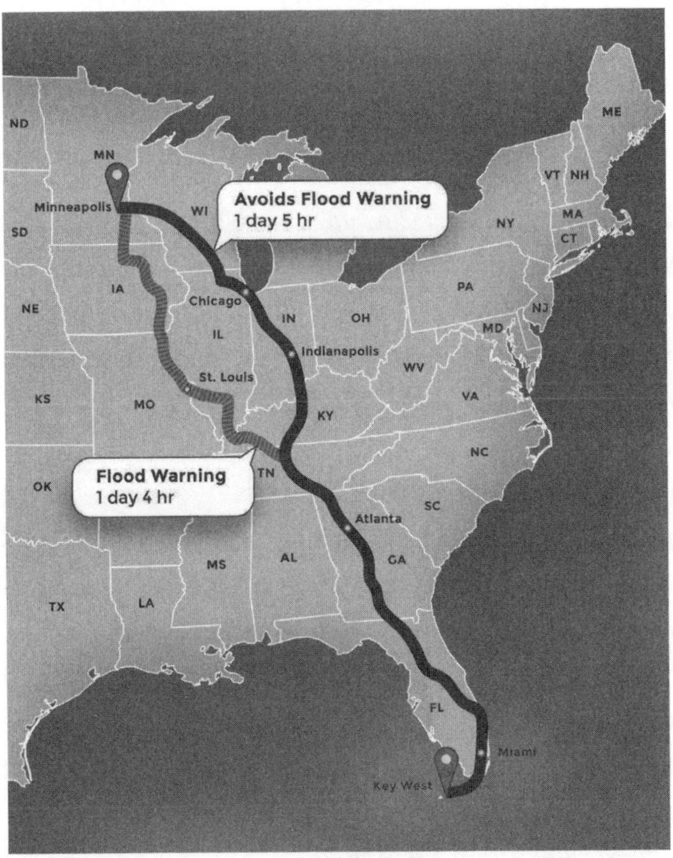

Figure 2.1. A map of my journey if I missed my flight and had to Uber.

With that soul-crushing picture in my mind, the story that bombarded my head took the unpreferred reality of locking my keys in the car from a small spark into a full-blown mental forest fire.

My thinking shifted to this: *I just literally ruined my whole life! I am completely doomed and may have just ended my speaking career. I swear this stuff only happens to me. If I didn't have bad luck, I wouldn't have any luck at all! This is the way it happens. Right when life gets rolling along, something ridiculous blows it all up!*

A downward spiral took my thinking from panic to blame: *These rental cars always have software that is decades behind. This stuff would never happen if they cared about their customers. Who designs these safety checks, and how did the entire team not think about this possibility?*

My ego ran wild, piling on judgments, critiques, stories, and assignments of motive. My thinking jumped to the future: *How am I going to tell the team? What a disaster. How are we going to clean up this mess after disappointing the client? This will surely ruin the client's event that they've worked so hard to set up.*

With these scattered and judgmental thoughts crashing together in my head, I realized that time was still ticking, and I needed to act. In my anxiety-filled decision-making, the only action that came to me was to call my wife and unload a combination of venting, complaining, and excuse making, which hopefully would end with her having a miracle idea to solve the issue.

Luckily, just prior to making that call, the steps of The Call to Greatness Framework hit me. Action taken with unclean thinking is often next wrong action, and that was exactly what I was about to do by burning more time helplessly commiserating with my wife on my predicament.

I took a deep breath and allowed the Edit Your Story tool to support me in cleaning up my thinking and, hopefully, revealing a more helpful next right action. Getting to the facts of what I knew for sure, my unpreferred reality landed as follows:

- I locked my keys in the back of my rental car.
- I feel terrified about missing the last flight out of Key West.
- I have an hour to get to an airport that is twelve minutes away.
- Based on what locals tell me, the Key West airport is quick to get through.
- I am scheduled to be on stage at 9:00 a.m. tomorrow in Minneapolis.

This quick, in-the-moment exercise allowed enough space to put aside *I've ruined my career* and freed space for next right action to appear. After only a few seconds, I didn't even have to ask, *What can I do to help?* From a place of clean thinking, possibilities to figure out my challenge began flowing. Without the ego's story creating a self-imposed blockage, innovation and problem-solving came naturally.

I did a search on my phone for "locksmith near me," quickly found three options, and dialed the first. As the phone rang, another next right action idea was to search for the best way to break a car window as I scanned the gravel parking lot for a big-enough rock. My next step would be to reach out to the team to search for possible late-night flights from the nearest larger airport so I could possibly make it to Minneapolis in time for my keynote.

Thankfully, the locksmith picked up and said, "I can be there in fifteen minutes."

The locksmith came straight over and had the car unlocked in two minutes. I thanked him profusely, and I made my flight with a few minutes to spare.

Watch for the Story Underneath

The Edit Your Story tool reveals solid initial action steps, but often people will find reasons not to follow through. This might be because a second story overrides the clarity of completing the first story. Those stories need editing too.

For example, a manager might say, "I'm clear about the feedback I need to give, but I know that when I bring it up, he's going to react badly. It will hurt our relationship. That could hurt the entire department and make things even worse." In this case, the ego has created a second layer of story about how someone might react to keep you from taking the right action. In this example, the second story robs someone of honest feedback and a great developmental opportunity. People are in charge of their own emotional welfare. Don't let a second story about how they might react derail the next helpful action.

When this pattern happens, I recommend following the simple directions that Edit Your Story has provided for you, even with the uncertainty of what could happen next. Trust next right action that comes to you after sizing up the facts on the paper. If that story is proving to be too strong for you to move into action, I recommend continuing through the remaining steps of The Call to Greatness Framework to clarify your space for impact even further. The action steps you land on at the completion of all tools of the framework are often even more deliberate and beneficial to the challenge you are addressing.

Have a Backup Plan, and Know Your Exit Line

From time to time, the Edit Your Story tool, as well as the additional tools you'll discover ahead, may create a reflection that can bump up against disgruntled egos in participants. If there is prolonged silence or you sense the temperature of the room or meeting reaching a boiling point, default to a rehearsed sentence or two that allows you to sideline a tool temporarily without losing the progress in starting The Call to Greatness Framework.

A mentor of mine once shared that you'll never fear a coaching moment or tough conversation if you know how to quickly get out of it. This is why in the approach outlined in this book, the visual RBL tools paired with your own unique memorized "exit line" are foundational to leading.

A personal favorite exit line of mine is, "Team <or team member>, great work on this so far—solid reflections! Let's go ahead and table this for now and head to the next item on the agenda. I'd love for you to work through this tool that we've started for a day or two, and we'll come back to this in our next <meeting, check-in, huddle, etc.>."

Another exit line I like is, "I appreciate your participation; you're giving me a lot to think about with this. Let's take a pause on this for now, and I'll send it out for us all to reflect on for the next few days. We'll move to the next action item and return to this conversation, possibly <insert time>."

Your exit line creates some breathing room while allowing the reflection that has begun from the tool to marinate. Because each tool is visual on paper, PowerPoint, PDF, or spreadsheet, you can simply resurface the tool in the next interaction that makes sense.

Sometimes, even with cleaned up thinking, the problem can be trickier and more complex than the Edit Your Story tool can sort through on its own. In those cases, it's time to move to the next step: finding your part in the issue. With your team clean in their thinking about the unpreferred reality, the next two steps of The Call to Greatness Framework set the stage for taking next right action. The first step involves a scan back at what may be your team's part in the situation, while the second calls for determining each person's role in the solution moving forward.

CHAPTER 3

CALL TO GREATNESS STEP 3. FIND YOUR PART: THE ACCOUNTING FOR TOOL

Clean thinking is transformative.

It was Einstein who said, "If I had an hour to solve a problem, I would spend fifty-five minutes defining it and five minutes finding the solution." When we spend the time stripping away the drama and untrue stories we tell ourselves about the unpreferred reality, what often emerges is a clear path forward—even in the most challenging circumstances. The Edit Your Story tool serves as a powerful first step, helping leaders validate experiences while inviting teams to reconsider the interpretations and assumptions that may be making the problem worse. For many situations, this tool alone can shift people from victimhood to problem-solving almost immediately, but it's not always enough to get to the best steps to take.

The Challenge of Initial Clarity

When people achieve this initial clarity through the Edit Your Story tool, they typically respond in one of two ways.

First, riding this surge of newfound clarity, people often jump into action. For many situations, this works out fine. However, in my experience, solid next steps often become *great* next right actions with a little more time through The Call to Greatness Framework. Making the extra effort of taking the problem at hand through the remaining steps and tools in this book builds heightened perspective of the entirety of the problem and leads to sharper and more intentional decisions. Think of it as a single tool getting you a solid score on the dartboard and the occasional bullseye, while the full Call to Greatness Framework lands you consistently on that coveted triple twenty.

Second, another more subtle phenomenon can occur. People become skilled at identifying problems and proposing solutions through the Edit Your Story process, but they struggle with follow-through. In fact, some individuals become so adept at articulating problems that this skill becomes another place to hide and another way to avoid taking action. They master the art of problem outlining without ever stepping into true accountability and the act of problem-solving.

THE SEESAW EFFECT OF BLAME AND HEROICS

Beyond just allowing people to hide behind problem identification, the clarity in their thinking leaves them or their team justified in the fact that the problem they are now pulled into wasn't their fault in the first place. From there, the natural temptation is to drift into blame and finger-pointing.

The focus becomes less on getting the situation back on track and more on the following:

- "Whose fault is it that this problem exists in the first place?"
- "Why the heck is this even an issue?"
- "This situation shouldn't be happening in the first place."
- "Why are we being pulled into this mess?"
- "Well, this wasn't our fault, and these circumstances are beyond our control and should be dealt with by someone else."

Even the groups I work with that are disciplined in not playing the blame game in this way can venture down this unhelpful path. When faced with an unpreferred work reality, most humans default to sidestepping personal accountability by blaming other people or their circumstances for why they can't succeed. They point to someone who didn't do their job, people who fell short of their commitments, or the circumstances that were too complex and difficult to navigate.

From this space, people then mentally step down, begin BMW (bitching, moaning, and whining) driving, and invest their energy in finger-pointing and blame or in daydreaming about having a different or better reality. They get stuck in inaction. If this predictable mental cycle is consistently enabled by leaders, people become even more frustrated and unable or unwilling to step into the place of impact where they can help.

When these beliefs or questions take root, another common reaction is to move quickly into heroics, making diving catches or engaging in proverbial firefighting. They begrudgingly take on the issue, begin overfunctioning, and end up putting the success of the situation on their shoulders. They muscle through to fix the problem and seesaw back and forth between blaming others for being pulled in to deal with unpreferred realities and simultaneously being the team that gets to "save the day" and get things back on track.

While this can be invigorating and alleviates the surface-level issue in the short term, if it becomes the standard, it often leads to fatigue and resentments toward other teams and departments in the long term.

Worse yet, teams that operate in this cycle risk becoming the righteous high performers who claim, "We have to do everything around here" or "This place would fall apart without us" while others are allowed to not pull their weight. The role of martyr becomes their identity and fuels unnecessary drama in the long run. After all, the most emotionally expensive employee is a high performer who is constantly in judgment of others they could be helping.

THE LEADERSHIP CHALLENGE AND WHERE ENABLING COMES IN

Leaders play the biggest part in all of this when they enable employees to not make conscious choices and allow the blame game to fester. This enabling erodes personal accountability over time and prevents teams from reaching next right action.

But what is the big deal with a little enabling here and there? Here is the real-world impact of enabling. Enabling shows up in debriefs when teams fall short of their goals or promises they've made to their customers, external partners, or patients. It sounds like, "Well, when you consider the competing priorities and the challenges in partnering with cross-functional teams in a matrixed environment, I suppose we did pretty well, considering the circumstances." Can you hear the subtle lowering of the standard and the bargain being made with accountability? **Every time you lower a standard, you set a new standard.**

Leaders enable people when they give bonus points for circumstances. Doing so creates an easy way out of accountability and leaves the group believing that the likelihood of future results depends on whether other people or circumstances become more ideal. Leaders enable circumstances to be the reason that their team can't succeed instead of the new reality in which they must succeed.

"MÁS DESPACIO POR FAVOR?"

This enabling has shown up in my own life. For years, I've tried to learn Spanish to better connect with my wife's family, who live in Spain. Every summer when we visit family in Spain, I recommit to finally improving my Spanish. If my wife needs to step away or I'm out running errands without her, I am forced to communicate in the language without the crutch of her quick translations. If I need something, I must look up phrases I don't know. If I miss part of a conversation, I must ask for it to be repeated or slowed down.

When I am on my own, I make progress and become more fluent. When my wife is around, if I get stuck on a word, I immediately default to her to provide the translation. After a while, my temptation is to forgo the effort altogether by speaking to her in English and having her translate. The more she enables me, the more I notice I take her up on it. At the end of the day, I am stunted in my growth with Spanish, and she is constantly interrupted with my (unpaid) translation requests.

This is the lesson inherent in the pattern of enabling. Both sides end up losing in the end. When leaders truly take a step back to see how much they are enabling their team, they see just how much it erodes accountability and fogs up available next right actions to help.

MOVING BEYOND BLAME TO PERSONAL ACCOUNTABILITY

With these common obstacles that can arise when seeking clarity about a problem, this next step of The Call to Greatness Framework is not so much about playing detective to determine whose fault it is that we are in the tough situation or what circumstances are causing it; it's about acknowledging whether there is any part you or your team are playing in the issue thus far.

Split up the word *accountability*, and you're left with *account* and *ability*. It's the simplest definition, because personal accountability is just that—the ability to account for your actions and how you got to where you are in a situation.

Accountability is a mindset, not a skill set. It is the core belief that you can have impact in a situation, that you're not at the mercy of your circumstances, and that there is always one action you can take to help, even in an unpreferred reality.

A mindset of personal accountability is cultivated through four essential factors:

1. **Commitment:** The willingness to do what it takes to get the results being sought (as long as those actions, of course, are legal, ethical, do not hurt anyone, etc.).
2. **Resilience:** The ability to stay the course in the face of obstacles and setbacks (often by reaching out to your large network of positive relationships and connections for tips to overcome the barrier).
3. **Ownership:** The acceptance of the consequences of your actions—good or bad. The act of taking ownership should be conversational more often than confrontational. This factor involves a healthy sense of pride and guilt about the results achieved so far, about which one can clearly state, "Here is what I did that helped, and here's what I did that hindered."

4. **Continuous Learning:** The perspective to see success and failure as learning that fuels future success as well as bigger commitments moving forward.

With these four factors as an anchoring mindset that fuels personal accountability, here's where the research comes in. The biggest predictor of someone's happiness, engagement, and results in the workplace correlates with their accountability levels. In fact, your team's happiness and success are correlated not with their circumstances but with the amount of accountability they take for their circumstances.[5]

From Enabling to Taking Accountability for Your Part

If you can't account for how you got to an unpreferred reality, either through conscious choices or often unconscious enabling, you can't change it. If you cannot identify the beliefs, choices, assumptions, and actions that led you to where you are, you won't see how to adjust your approach going forward. This is true for both the good results you and your team are achieving as well as the less-than-stellar results you may be dealing with that require your leadership, like the situations we focus on in this book.

---

5 Dusanee Kesavayuth, Dai Binh Tran, Vasileios Kikos, "Locus of Control and Subjective Well-Being: Panel Evidence from Australia," *PLOS One* 17, no. 8 (2022), https://doi.org/10.1371/journal.pone.0272714; Thomas W. H. Ng, Kelly L. Sorensen, and Lillian T. Eby, "Locus of Control at Work: A Meta-Analysis," *Journal of Organizational Behavior* 27, no. 8 (2006): 1057–1087, https://doi.org/10.1002/job.416 (workplace example); Aqsa Kamran et al., "Effect of Locus of Control on Academic Achievement," *International Journal of Creative Research Thoughts* 12, no. 11 (2024), http://www.ijcrt.org/papers/IJCRT2411524.pdf (academics example); Joel T. Stout, "Goal Setting Strategies, Locus of Control Beliefs, and Personality Characteristics of NCAA Division IA Swimmers" (master's thesis, University of North Texas, December 1999), https://digital.library.unt.edu/ark%3A/67531/metadc2236/m2/1/high_res_d/Thesis.pdf (sports example).

Taking accountability for your part in the situation is about answering honestly and without defensiveness: *What is my contribution to this less-than-ideal situation we find ourselves in?*

Too many leaders enable their teams to skip this step or avoid this reflection and leave all involved to continue blaming other people or their circumstances. Leaders must be diligent in ensuring that their team doesn't breeze past taking accountability for their contribution to the problem. This is not simply turning the blame on yourself or your team while enabling others to not pull their weight or fulfill their end of the bargain. It is taking an honest look at what poor behaviors you may have enabled or actions you avoided taking that culminated in creating this unpreferred reality you're now facing.

Most simply, this step of the call to greatness is an honest reflection on the choices you did or didn't make that helped or hindered thus far. Where did you say yes when you really meant no? Where did you see a behavior or pattern that wasn't helpful but turned the other way or stayed silent?

ACCOUNTABILITY IS NOT A DIRTY WORD; IT'S THE PATH FORWARD

The unfortunate truth in this step of The Call to Greatness Framework is that often others *will* have dropped the ball, forgotten to do something they promised, or created an unexpected disruption to the team. The problem that needs addressing might not have been your team's fault, or its origins might have been out of their control, but nonetheless, they are now involved in making sure the issue has minimal disruption to the customers, patients, or clients you serve.

When I'm training groups in organizations, I often find them stuck in this predicament, and what intrigues me most is the shift that happens when I pose these questions: "I know you've shared, in elaborate detail, a list of how *everyone else* has failed us and caused this problem, but I'm curious whether *you've* contributed in any unhelpful way to where we are. Did someone notice something and not bring it up? Did you have a gut feeling that you stayed silent about? Did you have a doubt about the project and didn't check in?"

People who honestly consider these questions respond with, "Well, I suppose there *were* a few times my instincts were telling me to speak up in the meeting or connect with someone to clarify my concern, but I didn't. I suppose that *may* have contributed to this current messy situation we're in." This often reveals an interesting truth: that **even when people have a good grasp of the facts of the problem, it doesn't mean they've accepted their part in contributing to it**.

While cleaning up thinking is about staying accountable to the truth and the facts of the situation, this step is about taking shared accountability for your part in that truth that has been revealed. As humans involved in an unpreferred reality, this subtle peek into our choices, assumptions, and behaviors that may have contributed to the situation can be uncomfortable. However, the initial discomfort and natural resistance of teams to dropping into personal accountability can be dissolved by working through the next RBL tool in The Call to Greatness Framework: the Accounting For tool.

USING THE ACCOUNTING FOR TOOL

The effectiveness of this tool lies in gently disrupting the blame cycle and helping to clearly audit each person's part in what has created the issue. This isn't about taking all the blame or enabling bad actors to wiggle out of their responsibilities. The tool is for engaging people so they begin to see what they can do to alter the situation for the better.

The Accounting For tool gives leaders a way to call a time-out and look back at any unaddressed lack of accountability that may be worsening the situation. At the same time, Accounting For reduces a leader's temptation to enable their team to simply blame other people or circumstances instead of engaging in honest and wholehearted problem-solving.

When something isn't going as expected or there is the risk of missing a deadline or goal, suddenly everyone becomes an expert at explaining why it's not their fault. You often hear countless reasons for why their hands are tied, how others have failed them, or how the issues are simply above their pay grade.

While it is completely natural and human to feel defensive when things go awry and focus the blame on external factors such as others' actions or intentions, challenging circumstances, limited resources, or time constraints, the Accounting For tool is able to cut through the circus of possible excuses by narrowing in on one essential question: *What's your part in this?*

This tool is astonishingly simple, and that's exactly why it works.

ACCOUNTING FOR TOOL: WHAT'S YOUR PART IN IT?

1. To begin, set aside some time with your team to reflect on and answer the following questions about the unpreferred reality or challenge they are facing. Encourage the team to write down or document their answers if needed to prepare for sharing. It is more common, however, for this to be a facilitated conversation with the leader simply asking the questions one by one and letting their team respond verbally.

   Accounting For Tool Questions for Self-Reflection (and What to Watch For)

   - **What are the results thus far, and are we on track to achieving our goal?** This is a reality check of what the results *truly* are now in terms of progress. Watch for the lowering of standards, with people saying, "We're doing pretty good considering the circumstances."

- **What's happening right now with this situation?** Listen for untrue stories, judgments, speculation, assignments of motive, etc.
- **What's your part in what's happening? How have you personally contributed to or detracted from the results so far?** These responses should be *I* statements—not responses that use *we, they,* or *them* (e.g., "I chose," "I assumed," "I did," "I didn't," "I decided," or "I avoided").
- **What are you currently believing about this situation? How is this belief affecting your behavior, attitude, creativity, and choices?**
- **What are the facts? What do you know for sure in this moment?** These questions act as another round of cleaning up thinking that may be needed.
- **What can you do right now to help?** This must be first-person focused, within their space of impact. This cannot be about changing others, changing circumstances, or requiring additional resources.
- **What can you commit to in the future?** Write this down.

2. When everyone is done, have the team report their responses. Leaders and team members should listen carefully and call out any statements that deflect personal accountability or assign blame. Watch for statements that begin with *we, you,* or *they* instead of *I*. When heard, these can be respectfully called out with a reminder to start the sentence with, "I chose," "I assumed," or "I denied." Allow the person sharing to gather their thoughts and begin the response again but now anchored back into personal accountability.

continued

3. After everyone has shared insights, ensure that each person has clearly answered the question, "What are you committing to doing differently moving forward?" Capture the commitments in writing, and, for an added bonus, include a deadline when the individual feels it can be completed. The written commitments can, and should, be referred to in future check-ins and coaching.

Digital Toolkit: Want to get the digital download for this tool or the full Call to Greatness Framework Toolkit PDF? Scan the QR code here.

The power of the Accounting For tool is twofold: It helps leaders stop enabling their teams, and it brings the focus back onto each person's realm of impact to help the situation. Continuous learning is baked in because the commitments made can be used for ongoing personal development, which helps transform lack of progress or failures into better performance.

Now that you have the ground rules for using the Accounting For tool, let's look at a few examples in which leaders used it to stop enabling their teams, to cultivate accountability, and to support people in finding their space for impact.

THE FULL CALL TO GREATNESS IN ACTION—VIRAL ON TIKTOK

Having gained clarity in my thinking on the issue of reimagining our social media strategy just as it was taking off by completing the Edit Your Story tool, I knew I next needed to find my part in the situation. Grabbing a printout I had on my desk of the Accounting For tool, I silently ran through each question one by one. No more hiding from personal accountability. It was time to see what my part in this situation was thus far.

What were the results thus far, and were we on track to achieving our goal? It quickly became clear that we had two viral videos with millions of views. However, when I considered whether we were on track to achieving our goal, I reflected on our founder's objective regarding this video content on social media, which was to create more quality videos that were on message and on brand, especially for those viewers who would be hearing us for the first time. My focus, however, seemed to be on reach and the number of views of the video instead of her stated goal. So were we on track?

This reflection revealed that the team and I might not be.

What was happening right now with this situation? The Edit Your Story tool had helped reveal and make me aware of some of my judgments, speculations, and even assignments of motive.

With that, I moved on to consider the next question in the tool: **What was my part in what was happening? How had I personally contributed to or detracted from the results thus far?** This was a breakthrough. As I honestly considered this question, I had to come clean about the fact that I had noticed that one of the videos was gaining hundreds of thousands of views a few days prior. Although I had noticed a few negative comments, I had justified them by thinking that some people just wanted to be mean online and did not understand our message. I had thought that

continued

in any story told, someone would find an insult in it, so I had not thought much of it.

I had chosen not to communicate with our founder or the team about those initial messages I was seeing and my concerns. I realized that I had become wrapped up in our marketing partner's metrics of reach, in our increased views, and in creating attention-grabbing videos, missing the point that it might not have been the best introduction to that story or concept for a new audience. I had not called this out because I was focused on the number of views coming in.

Although a tough pill to swallow, this question pulled out some accountability I wanted to be shielded from.

What was I currently believing about the situation? As the Accounting For tool opened my eyes to some of my hidden underlying beliefs, I realized I wrongly believed that my preferred approach was the only way to capitalize on these big moments when a marketing effort was getting significant interactions. I had many stories and opinions that I was about to bring back to the meeting, which could contribute to more problems.

So **what could I do right then to help?** The first few things that came to mind were to continue through The Call to Greatness Framework. Although I had more insight about my part thus far in the unpreferred reality, I was still unclear about what to do in the short term to help, what to do once I returned to the meeting, and most important, what to do in the long term to help solve this problem with the team.

What was I committing to in this moment? I was committing to continuing The Call to Greatness Framework in the remaining time I had before the meeting started up again. I would also commit to keeping in mind some of the untrue stories and judgments I had jumped to when completing the Edit Your Story tool and stay intentional if those thoughts returned in the meeting. Lastly, I made a commitment in the moment to keep an eye on the goal of our founder for the social strategy and not fall back into my personal preferences and goals for the number of views on the videos.

The Accounting For tool showed me that I had refused to see my part in the issue and was only blaming our founder for what I perceived as a bad decision. But now that I knew how I had contributed to getting us here, it was time to determine my role in creating the solution by moving on to the next step in The Call to Greatness Framework.

It's All Their Fault!

A human resources consulting team took on the project of recruiting ten engineers to work in North Dakota during the region's historic oil boom. The group believed the goal was doable and was excited about the incentive of a bonus for each engineer hired. They committed to securing ten engineers in three months.

A month or so before the deadline, the team leader heard that seven of the ten engineers had been secured—70 percent of the goal. Wanting to support the project's final push, she called a meeting to get an update. The team members told her the project was going "pretty good." They'd been working hard, they said, generating a lot of activity and stirring up interest in the positions. Mirroring the enthusiasm of the group, the leader said, "Wow, so we have seven engineers signed up with a month left? Sounds like we are on target!"

After an awkward silence, a team member corrected, "Well, actually, we have seven people *interested* in the position." The leader, realizing that zero engineers had been contracted with only four weeks until deadline, asked in horror, "Why was the answer to my question 'pretty good' given the reality that we are not even close to delivering on our commitment?" She got a litany of not-my-fault responses.

One team member began, "Well, actually, this is marketing's issue because we met with them months back and they didn't get the website officially up until a month into the project. We realized after the fact that the link to sign up for the opportunity was broken, so we have no idea how many people clicked through who were interested in the opportunity! Also, as you know, I can't really control marketing, and it was really their terrible planning and execution that doomed us from the start."

The next person jumped in with their reasoning: "I met with senior leaders about what we were trying to do, and when we had social events for these engineers to come in and learn about the opportunity, they mostly small-talked about sports, weather, or recent global events. They didn't really do a great job of selling the positions or discussing the upside and possibilities. Don't they get paid the big money, and shouldn't they be good at doing this sort of thing?"

The third person rode the momentum of the blame train and added, "Did you realize how harsh the winters up in North Dakota are? They are absolutely brutal! I heard that some months, you have to walk backwards with your hood up just to get through the frigid wind! This has been a big negative for each person we are trying to sign up."

As the team leader took these responses in, it became glaringly obvious the team was assigning the bulk of the blame to the marketing team, senior leaders, and North Dakota winters while skillfully brushing past their part in the lack of progress thus far in the success of the project. To make matters worse, there was a month remaining before the hiring deadline, and not a single suggestion had been uttered for how to get everything back on track. They viewed getting results as dependent on having a completely different reality and blamed circumstances for their lack of success.

It was time to venture into the next step of the call to greatness. Passing out a printed Accounting For tool to each team member, the leader began by validating the team's experience: "I can hear that many of you are frustrated with some of our partners involved with this project and that conditions have been challenging for achieving our desired results." Then she invited the team to reconsider the sense they were making of their current results (i.e., failures of the marketing team, socially inept senior leaders, and cold weather) and move into the call to greatness.

The leader began with a brief Edit Your Story tool to clean up some of the group's unhelpful thinking. In doing so, the team was able to refocus on the real problem at hand (i.e., zero secured candidates) while dissolving some lingering judgments and assignments of motive toward the senior leaders in marketing that, whether the group liked it or not, would be the only team available to help them achieve their goal moving forward. Even with this heightened clarity, the leader noticed the conversation drift back into subtle excuses and finger-pointing. Calling a time-out, she referred to the printout with the Accounting For tool questions and invited each team member to spend a moment reflecting on each question to honestly account for their part in the results thus far.

After team members completed the exercise, she asked them to share responses, and she noticed a profound shift.

The first team member began, "I chose not to put a project plan together. I held a quick meeting with the marketing department about the website, and I didn't follow up. In fact, they seemed a little unclear on what I needed, but I chose not to check in. When I heard some feedback that the link to apply was redirecting candidates, I assumed marketing would take care of it instead of ensuring myself that it was working."

In jumped the second team member: "I assumed senior leaders knew how to recruit and it would come naturally to them. I chose not to brief them on what good recruiting looks like in a social situation. I didn't provide speaking points for them to use at the social gatherings. I also didn't give feedback after the first event we hosted to help leaders sell the position more effectively."

The one who had mentioned the weather raised his hand and simply said with some rosy cheeks and a somewhat embarrassed smirk on his face, "My apologies for using the weather that we already knew about in that part of the country as my excuse." He thanked the leader for the Accounting For tool and getting everyone back on track.

After thanking individuals for participating, the leader emphasized that progress with the tool required the team to not only see their part in the problem but also commit to changes in their approach that would help them achieve the desired results.

With the work of the Accounting For tool nearly done, the first team member jumped in and said, "I will commit to following up with marketing this afternoon and resetting priorities with the team. I also commit to reviewing my process for project plans and will ensure we create and follow it in the future." This was music to the leader's ears.

It turns out that shared accountability can be contagious. The next team member followed shortly after with commitments: "I promise to set clearer expectations with senior leaders on their role at recruiting social events in the future. I will connect with them prior and do some role-playing, and I'll provide some speaking points that they can use to really sell the opportunity to candidates. Since we have an upcoming event and still a month to recruit, I will get started on this tomorrow morning."

Several team members followed with similar personal commitments and changes in their approach, and off they went. The realizations and course corrections made in this meeting helped the team secure eight of the ten engineers promised by the deadline. While the results fell short of the ultimate goal, the team's measure of success included a renewed clarity about how their intentional choices led to their results and how they could do it better next time. This lesson continued to fuel their resilience and continuous learning.

A Breakthrough Success Story Becomes Sustainable

A health-care leader I worked with told us the Accounting For tool helped her strengthen a culture of accountability. A member of her team had a pattern of saying yes during meetings and then proceeded to spend time in "meetings" after the meeting telling his colleagues why he wasn't on board with decisions or strategic initiatives. When he was invited to provide input on how to implement new strategies or policies during official meetings, he usually stayed silent.

The behavior persisted in the face of clear and specific feedback about the employee's unprofessional and unhelpful actions. After a year, the leader chose not to enable the employee, and the employee ultimately left the organization.

When the news spread that the colleague was leaving, the leader noticed that morale on the team immediately improved. She saw a renewed sense of energy for the work they were doing. Team members thanked the leader for *finally* having the courage to remove a toxic coworker.

This sounds like a leadership success story, but the leader couldn't see it that way. She couldn't help but think of the question, *What was each of our parts in the unpreferred reality we had been facing with this colleague?* She used an analogy of having treated the virus without immunizing the team and decided to use the Accounting For tool to help the team members see their contributions in enabling the culture to get off track.

Handing out the questions, she validated the experience that the team had, in fact, gone through a challenging time with the departed colleague. Then she invited them to the reflection questions of the tool to see what insights they might be leaving on the table from the experience.

She asked people to reflect deeply on their contributions to the dynamics of the situation. Where had they stepped down instead of up? Had they stayed silent when they could have spoken up? Had they believed stories that kept them from supporting the organization and the strategies? Had they colluded with their colleague to simply avoid conflict?

People said things such as, "Even when he openly said he wasn't aligned with our strategy, I chose to stay silent and to just work around him" and "I chose to not speak up in the meeting and address the comments I found unhelpful, and then I talked poorly about him behind his back."

After the exercise, each team member (including the leader) could more clearly see their accountability deficits. The reflections gave the team insight into what kind of culture they wanted to create, codified with practical, written commitments to the choices they would make to prevent an all-too-common workplace dynamic to repeat itself.

In one statement, a team member said, "I am committing to be a good advocate for our team and the culture we've created, and I will be diligent about speaking up if someone is moving into that type of drama pattern." Another wrote, "I will commit to moving beyond my default to avoid conflict in meetings and not participate in meetings after the meeting. I also will support my colleagues when they have the courage to do so."

Doing the Accounting For tool had, in fact, immunized the team alongside the treatment of the cultural "virus." Taking the time to complete the tool had given everyone a heightened awareness of how they contributed to the problem in the past and now clarity on how they could avoid creating the same workplace culture issue in the future.

USING HOPE AS THEIR STRATEGY

While the Accounting For tool is a secret weapon for helping teams drop into accountability and make intentional choices to get things back on track, it can be used just as effectively to ensure that teams aren't simply using hope as their strategy when they are achieving good results. In other words, it can ensure that your team can account for the habits, decisions, and choices that are contributing to success that you want to *continue* in the future.

At a break during a session I was conducting, I overheard an executive from the marketing team at a beauty retailer share, "I saw the latest numbers and projections, and I'm not sure what is happening, but we are really ahead of things at this point in the year. Now, I don't want to say much more because I don't want to jinx it, but typically, it isn't looking quite like this during this season."

This immediately jumped out to me as an opportunity to invite the key individuals involved with those great initial results to clean up thinking and venture into the Accounting For tool to discover what intentional choices, decisions, or processes were producing these great results. With this insight and understanding, the group could not only continue doing what they now *knew* was working; they could share that information with others.

In completing the tool in a follow-up session, the group was able to get past their ungrounded superstition that they might jinx the promising results they had been achieving and move from guessing at what *might* work to committing to next right action that they *knew* worked. Best of all, they were able to return to the tool later in the year, when they started to notice the numbers slipping in the wrong direction, to make new choices to get them back on track.

If you've made it this far through The Call to Greatness Framework, your team is most likely experiencing profound clarity on not only what the problem is but also their contribution to it thus far. From here, it may feel like you are holding back racehorses in the starting gate, ready to surge into action, as they wait for the gates to fly open. The time for that sprint forward into action is almost here, but one more step is required before it is optimal to pick next right actions. This involves helping your team know the role they can play in the solution and what it means to buy into it. Before going there in the next chapter, let's review what to watch out for as you use the Accounting For tool, as well as common situations in which you'll want to invite your team to complete it.

WHAT TO WATCH FOR

When completing the Accounting For tool with your team, you may encounter moments that feel unproductive or stalled. Here are some insights into what may actually be happening beneath the surface.

- The ego attempts to wiggle out of accountability at all times because it likes to remain the victim of the situation. This tool gives a victim mindset nowhere to hide.
- Know that silence is needed with this tool. The ego tries to avoid self-reflection at all costs. Ask the questions; then, let them linger and do their work.
- Trust the reflection questions from the Accounting For tool that turn the team inward, as opposed to the typical tactics of the ego that try to look outward to blame other people and circumstances.
- The tool shouldn't overrotate into shame or beating yourself up, as if every issue is your team's fault alone or that you can control all outcomes. The experience of the tool should feel balanced, with a hint of discomfort as the ego settles into personal accountability and comes clean about its contribution to the situation.

- The tool isn't meant to be weaponized and used for interrogating your team. The idea is to provide a structured template to drop into personal accountability and discuss what each person has been doing to help or hinder progress in the situation.

COMMON SITUATIONS IN WHICH THE ACCOUNTING FOR TOOL IS NEEDED

Use this tool when you observe any of the following dynamics on your team:

- When employees or teams are blaming, finger-pointing, or not accepting responsibility for their actions
- When you hear us-versus-them language when it comes to a problem that needs to be addressed for your customers, clients, or patients
- When your team often takes the stance as the innocent ones who had nothing to do with the issue at hand
- When you notice your team is enabling others to continue to engage in behaviors that aren't helpful to strengthening teamwork, maintaining professionalism, or working toward organizational results
- When your team is quick to jump in and "save the day" in the short term but doesn't reflect further on why problems consistently come up that take heroic scrambles or diving-catch efforts (the tool helps teams more deeply contemplate what they could do in the midterm and long term to improve processes or address the patterns leading to the unpreferred reality showing up)
- When a team is experiencing promising results but doesn't seem to know why or how they are doing it

- When it feels as if people are using hope as their strategy or not following a process, methodology, or intentional approach to achieving consistent results

CHAPTER 4

CALL TO GREATNESS STEP 4. KNOW YOUR ROLE: THE ORGANIZATIONAL ALIGNMENT AND BUY-IN DECISION TABLE

As your team combines newfound clarity for their part in the situation with their cleaned up thinking about the problem, something powerful begins to emerge: a growing sense of agency. Team members start to recognize where and how they can contribute meaningfully to the solution. This is the momentum that naturally builds when people discover their space of impact.

The first two tools in The Call to Greatness Framework have already set your team on a promising path. The helpful ideas revealed in the Accounting For tool have them leaning toward effective action.

If acted on, the commitments from the tool will no doubt hit near the center of the dartboard and produce the occasional bullseye in terms of next right action. However, taking the time to complete the remaining steps of The Call to Greatness Framework guarantees that what your team does next is even more precise and hits that coveted triple-twenty score.

Pulling this off consistently requires the next step of The Call to Greatness Framework, which helps your team to clearly understand and buy into their specific roles in the solution.

Got Your Part; Now Find Your Role

Just because people have now taken accountability for their part in the issue doesn't necessarily mean they are clear on their role in moving toward the solution. Sometimes they have not yet accepted and bought in to taking action in the role the situation is calling on them to play. This is precisely the next place people get stuck.

You will struggle to find someone experiencing more grueling suffering at work than the employee who is constantly (and often unknowingly) trying to contribute in the wrong role for what the situation merits. To the same effect, there is no more detrimental source of drama that exists than a leader who enables those they lead to not know their role and where they can best help and engage in solutions.

You will recognize this in your team immediately when there is constant confusion and questioning about what needs to be done, who is responsible for doing it, or, in the worst cases, whether it even needs to be done in the first place. These questions often indicate that the team does not understand how to find their role in moving toward the solution and is experiencing ambiguity about their responsibilities.

It is a dead giveaway that this is happening when you overhear classic statements such as the following:

"That's above my pay grade."

"That's why they get paid the big bucks."

"If I ran the place, stuff like this would never happen."

Or another crowd favorite, "If they would just ask the people closest to the work before making these decisions, we'd never be in this predicament."

Each of these statements is an immediate warning sign of a team that is engulfed in ambiguity about the roles they need to play in moving through this particular unpreferred reality. The problem with ambiguity of this sort is that it doesn't just invite conflict; it exponentially manufactures it.

Ambiguity within a team doesn't just confuse; it creates a disorienting version of organizational whiplash that leaves teams unable to align their efforts. Ambiguity creates either total chaos, with everyone frantically working out of position, or complete stagnation, with capable talent standing idle, unsure where to plug in. When this is unaddressed in teams, it creates a maddening cycle of false progress, like two people strapped to the same bungee cord, sprinting in opposite directions only to be violently snapped back to where they started. Everyone appears busy, and everyone feels exhausted, but nothing actually moves forward.

To move from ambiguity (and avoid the mess outlined above), it is essential for leaders to create clarity. But clarity in what areas?

The Root Cause of All Conflict in the Workplace

Nearly all conflict in the workplace can be traced to a fundamental lack of clarity in three critical areas: goals, roles, and procedures. When your team is crystal clear on each of these elements, they unlock the endless potential of a team that is in perfect alignment with their organization. If left unclear, eventually people can hide out in resistance because a dense mental fog remains as to the why of the organization's goals, who is responsible for accomplishing them, and how exactly the work should be done.

In the worst cases of this unaddressed ambiguity, teams that haven't clarified goals, roles, and procedures spend countless hours clogged up in meetings in which nearly every level of the organizational hierarchy, from frontline staff to CEO, converge to make even the most inconsequential decision for the business. This ends up resembling a youth soccer match in which five-year-olds swarm around the ball, fighting for possession with no understanding of spacing, position, or purpose. It is the proverbial huddle ball. Even trivial issues seem insurmountable to move beyond when this is happening.

If this sounds like one of your recent meetings, then suffer no longer.

The goals, roles, and procedures concept is your starting point as a leader to begin clearing this up.

GOALS

Essential question: What are we hoping to accomplish, and by when?

A lack of clarity or alignment on goals causes people to work against each other without realizing it.

Simple examples of common business goals are increasing revenue, improving safety or outcomes, building brand, increasing patient or client experience scores, remaining compliant, increasing efficiency, and decreasing costs.

Some people might have no idea what the main goals or priorities are, let alone how their efforts can support those goals. Don't take for granted that everyone is on the same page, and clarify goals by doing the following:

- Remind your team often of key priorities, change initiatives, and organizational goals.
- Keep these goals as visual as possible for your team by creating a dashboard or another way to track progress and results.
- Whenever possible, leaders should connect each change or decision that is made back to the core goals of the organization.
- The goal clarification could also link to the organization's mission, vision, and values.
- This can also be a great connection point to why this decision is happening and how it settles within the why of the organization's existence.

ROLES

Essential questions: Who is going to do what on our team? What is expected of me, and what can I depend on others to do? What is my role in decision-making?

Conflict disperses in all directions when team members are confused about roles. When clarifying roles, most people default to job descriptions. However, looking to job outlines for what employees were initially hired to do isn't enough. Job descriptions can't capture all that may come up in a position, they are always changing, and people's interpretations of them often vary. Each person's role (as opposed to their job description) is to fulfill the mission and strategies set by the organization within legal, moral, and ethical bounds.

With that said, leaders must evolve their team members' understanding of how to fulfill their individual roles in the modern workplace. RBL has delineated three roles that people can play at work when they are trying to make progress on an issue. It's critical for you as a leader to clarify which role your team is being asked to play in the current unpreferred reality. All of us will play all three of these roles in different situations and at different times in our careers. The problem, in terms of successfully answering the call to greatness or missing it, comes when people are playing (or enabled to play) the wrong role for what the situation merits.

Let's overview the available roles one by one.

1. **Decision-Maker:** This person or group of people, typically at the highest level of an organization, can say yes or no to the overall strategy, change initiatives, and shift the direction of the business. Depending on the structure of the organization, decision-makers generally make up around 1 percent of the organization. They have the authority and responsibility to make the decision, to assign resources, and to start or stop big initiatives.

   If you find yourself wondering, *Am I the decision-maker on this?* you've just discovered you probably aren't. Decision-makers nearly always know that they are decision-makers.

   While many people believe *those* decision-makers are a person, or select group, who pulls all the strings of the business, the reality is that external factors outside the metaphorical walls of the organization often drive the direction of business decisions. Examples might include changing marketplace dynamics, regulations, competition, technology advances, supply-chain issues, competitive pressures, and so on.

   It's likely that several of these factors simultaneously intersect to influence organizational decisions and the changes being called for in your workplace. Depending on the forces in play, the highest-level decision-makers in the organization respond as best they can with the information they have. Understanding this can help people to realize that it isn't just "leaders" or "decision-makers" dreaming up mandates out of nowhere. More likely they are responding to the ever-changing shifts in the marketplace that are affecting the business.

If you're not a decision-maker involved in the situation, you might be getting called on to play the role of a consultant.

2. **Consultant:** Consultants don't decide or tell people what to do. They let decision-makers know what they could do given the goals they are trying to achieve. They offer the options or possible pathways to achieve those goals and outline the associated costs, benefits, and risks of each approach. True consultants don't get to make the decision. The moment a consultant says, "The only way to do this is . . ." or "What you should do is . . ." they have moved out of the consultant role and are trying to drive the decision, which will lead to drama and role confusion. Instead, consultants wait for the path chosen by the final decision-maker(s) and, once decided, fully buy in to start executing the plan.

   If you haven't been asked to come to the table as a consultant, one possible role remains.

3. **A Good Person to Be Informed:** By process of elimination, if the first two roles aren't what you're being asked to contribute, given the unpreferred reality, you've been tasked with being a Good Person to Be Informed of the decision. Feel that. For many, landing in this role initially feels unsettling because it seems oddly passive, as if surrendering a power they've always possessed in their organization.

   While this role is less involved in decisions and *what* is to be done, it is heavily influential in *how* the decision is executed. In practical terms, one loosens their grip on the need to control major strategic decisions and instead realizes that their greater contribution lies in the countless incremental choices they make to achieve the goal or deliver on the strategy. In this apparent surrendering, one reclaims the decision-making power they *actually* have instead of lusting for that which they *wish* they had. For this reason, the role of a Good Person to Be Informed is an active role that adds value to an organization equal to that of the other possible roles one can play.

A Good Person to Be Informed is the most common organizational role, and, in fact, it is arguably the most essential role because even the best decisions can't reach their potential if those executing them are halfhearted in their buy-in and efforts. Once you're able to settle wholeheartedly into this role when it is yours to play, you unlock exponential potential to make all the little decisions along the way to achieve the hoped-for goals.

Before anyone proceeds in any role, but especially in this execution-focused one, you should of course consider whether what is being suggested or asked of you is illegal, immoral, unethical, or alienating a population your organization serves. Assuming it passes that test, your next move should be to wholeheartedly buy in to execute the idea and mitigate any risks you see along the way.

Someone who is skillful at being a Good Person to Be Informed doesn't expend energy fighting for the wrong role or arguing with reality. They are skillful at greeting decisions with, "Wow, good to know" or "Thank you for letting me know." This can be followed by, "I'm in with the goal and what we are doing. Now let's talk about how, given some concerns and risks I have identified, my expertise can help us get there."

Most roles can be clarified by reflecting on whether you are a decision-maker, a consultant, or a Good Person to Be Informed of a decision. This is where most people get stuck in stepping fully into their space for impact and, eventually, next right action. Making assumptions about roles can lead to conflict or inaction, whereas discussing roles openly helps get everyone in alignment.

PROCEDURES

Essential question: How will we best work together efficiently?

Once teams are clear on goals, know how they fit into the organization's strategies, and have a solid understanding of their roles, procedures outline how teams are going to best get work done together.

Clarity about procedures doesn't only reduce conflict; it ensures efficient use of resources on a team. If you want efficiency in the workplace, standardized processes are your friend because they free people up for higher-level work. In general, aim to automate nearly everything you get your hands on that equates to lower-value work.

Great teams don't require hundreds of procedures; they operate on a handful of agreed-on nonnegotiables. Examples of nonnegotiables within procedures include adhering to standardized processes, using internal software or checklists, following evidence-based methodologies, and complying with regulations or best-practice approaches. In some organizations, procedures may also include following workflows, reporting procedures, or coordinating the group's efforts in other agreed-on ways.

Once they have set procedures, leaders must make sure to not negotiate the nonnegotiables. This sounds obvious, but it's where most teams fail. The very purpose of making something nonnegotiable is that it shouldn't have to be negotiated anymore, yet in my consulting work, I see teams constantly pressured to make exceptions. Every request sounds reasonable in isolation: "Just this once," "We're kind of special over here," "Can't we bend the rules for this client?" But each exception diminishes the efficiency that following a nonnegotiable grants. When leaders consistently protect their nonnegotiables from being rehashed, they preserve the mental bandwidth and decision-making energy that gets wasted in endless case-by-case negotiations. The nonnegotiable becomes a decision made once that eliminates thousands of future decisions.

The beauty of this approach is that most leaders only need seven to ten nonnegotiables when it comes to procedures to create profound clarity on how 90 percent of work will get done with their team. In the remaining 10 percent of cases in which these nonnegotiables or processes fall short in catching a problem, team members can jump in to use their individual resiliency to save the experience or help the customer. They can use the opportunity to add their own personal touch to the customer experience and tap into their unique skill sets and creativity to facilitate a memorable human-centered interaction that solves the issue and ultimately sets your organization apart in the marketplace.

When overall goals are clear and team members know their roles and core procedures, it pays to be flexible as a leader regarding how people handle these outlier situations. This intentional flexibility ensures that teams avoid getting overproceduralized, when people feel the workplace is so rigid that they can't be themselves or authentic.

No Alignment? No Problem. The Tool for the Perfect Role Clarity and Buy-In

With this all said, the question becomes, *How do I best ensure that my team has alignment in goals, roles, and procedures and, most important, knows their role in solving the current unpreferred reality?*

This is where the next RBL tool comes in as support to quickly find which role those you lead need to settle into to best contribute to the solution. Using the tool ensures that your team is fully equipped to take the best action to proceed given the situation.

Whether your team has been thrown into a short-term unpreferred reality, a midterm unpreferred reality, or a long-term unpreferred reality, identifying and accepting the role each team member is asked to play are among the most critical elements of answering the call to greatness. When this is done well, your team can rest assured that their input, actions, and behaviors contribute to solutions. The RBL tool called the Organizational Alignment and Buy-In Decision Table will help you quickly reveal to your team, in a nonconfrontational way, whether they are acting in the appropriate role as they prepare to take next right action.

Completing this tool provides clarity and accountability about their specific role, gets teams behind organizational decisions, and inspires wholehearted action to make the organization's goals successful.

ORGANIZATIONAL ALIGNMENT AND BUY-IN DECISION TABLE

Before beginning this tool, I recommend printing out the table for each of your team members and having them answer each question as it guides them through the decision table. If the conversation is one-on-one, it is most effective to sit down with the printout, side by side with the person who is working to settle into their role, and to guide them through the questions. If the conversation is virtual, the tool can be screen-shared so the team can follow along visually. Some of the questions within the table may spark clarification questions and discussions. Welcome those, and refer to the preceding pages to define any roles or provide additional context.

continued

STEP 1	For this unpreferred reality, has the decision been made as to how to address it?	
1a	Yes, the decision has been made, and the situation must be addressed now.	Go to Step 2.
1b	No, the strategy and changes to address the situation are still being considered, and my input is needed.	Go to Step 3.
STEP 2	Is the decision illegal, unethical, immoral, or alienating a population or demographic your organization serves?	
2a	Yes, there is an objective reason this decision should not be made.	Great catch, and speak up immediately! It's something that might have been overlooked by those involved in the decision prior to you. Stop the action, and call out the issue.
2b	No, I have no objections that fit these criteria.	Go to Step 3.
STEP 3	Do you understand the role you are expected to play in working toward the solution? Recall that these roles include decision-makers, the people who can say yes or no to high-level strategies and changes; consultants, those who offer options and their associated risks; and a Good Person to Be Informed, which describes most of the people in an organization.	
3a	Yes, I understand the role I am expected to play, regardless of whether it's the role I prefer.	Go to Step 4.

3b	No, I'm unclear about my intended role in this situation.	Seek clarity from your leaders or team. Most people unsure of their role at this point will be a Good Person to Be Informed, but remember that this role is not passive, and it doesn't mean you can't offer feedback for what happens at your organization. All three roles have equal value within the organization. You may even ask, "Are you asking me to be a consultant in how to address this issue?" If you're wondering, *Am I the decision-maker here?* you most likely aren't, as decision-makers typically know they are decision-makers. Settle into your role given the situation, and go to Step 4.
STEP 4	Are you struggling to buy into the strategy, decision, or change, or are you still struggling to settle into your role and use your expertise to take next right action toward the organization's goals?	
4a	Yes, I am not fully on board with the organization's decision or the role they are expecting me to play.	Go to Step 5.
4b	No, I understand the organization's strategy and the role I'm needed to play.	Go to Step 6.
STEP 5	Do you see specific risks with the decision or strategy that are based on your expertise rather than your opinion? In general, expertise is most helpful and considers how something could work, while opinions focus on why it won't work. Consider the differences that follow before proceeding.	

continued

	OPINION Not relying on factual evidence or specialized knowledge Focused on personal preferences or beliefs Based solely on gut feelings, anecdotes, or speculation Reluctance to change because skill sets haven't been consistently updated Often includes conscious or unconscious biases Personal judgments, projections, or false interpretations Assumptions about or assignments of motive	**EXPERTISE** Based on data, research, evidence, policies, precedence, legislation, proven methodologies, case studies, and success stories Comes from training, education, or hands-on knowledge in specific areas Focused on what helps the potential of the business or organization Tends to capitalize on change by updating skill sets to help maintain readiness for what's next Includes input with heightened awareness of conscious or unconscious biases Information gathered and synthesized from experts, practitioners, and stakeholders Fact-based, observable behaviors and giving the benefit of doubt to others
5a	No, my concerns aren't based on expertise. The decision simply isn't my preference.	Remember, while personal opinions can reflect valid concerns, they tend to focus on "why we can't" rather than "how we could." Jot down these opinions or concerns that will be addressed when determining next right action. With those written down, go to Step 6.
5b	Yes, I see a list of the risks with this decision, change, or unpreferred reality that are based on expertise, and I'm ready to share them to be considered.	Document these concerns now; then go to Step 6.

STEP 6	Do you feel ready to align your efforts with your role and the organization's goal?	
6a	Yes, I am aligned with the organization's overarching goals and ready to provide my input and energy toward the solution.	Go to Step 7.
6b	No, there is too much of a gap between my expectations and those of the organization, and I'm unwilling to buy into focusing on how I could contribute given the circumstances.	Consider one last time whether there are risks or concerns you'd be willing to share that are holding back your buy-in and that your team could discuss so you can navigate moving forward. Could you document or share those? If you're unwilling to share or work through those with your colleagues, it might be time to consider transitioning off the team or possibly outside the organization, where you *can* better align with the strategies or decisions being made. The choice always lies with you about whether to stay in joy or leave in peace. Both are incredibly peaceful decisions, but trying to remain in the third option of staying and hating or resisting only sabotages your chances of contributing to organizational results and fuels personal discontent. Sitting in this third option is a stance that cannot be tolerated for both the success of the organization and for an individual's own long-term happiness. The best way to add value is to play your role fully. Doing so frees up energy for progress, collaboration, and impact.

continued

STEP 7	You're ready for next right action! Even if you have concerns, risks, or potential issues to be considered around the unpreferred reality being addressed or the organization's decision, your opportunity to convert those into constructive impacts on the solution will soon happen by completing the final step of The Call to Greatness Framework.

Digital Toolkit: Want to download this tool and get the printout to use it in your next meeting or coaching moment? Then follow the QR code below. You can also download the full Call to Greatness Toolkit.

THE FULL CALL TO GREATNESS IN ACTION—VIRAL ON TIKTOK

With newfound clarity on the unpreferred reality of our social media strategy disruption and my accountability in the situation, it was time to look at my role in the solution based on what seemed to be a new strategy moving forward. It was time for the Organizational Alignment and Buy-In Decision Table.

Thankfully, I still had ten minutes before our meeting resumed, giving me just enough time to complete the tool to clarify where I could best contribute moving forward.

STEP 1	For this unpreferred reality, has the decision been made as to how to address it?	
1a	Yes, the decision has been made, and the situation must be addressed now.	Go to Step 2.
1b	No, the strategy and changes to address the situation are still being considered, and my input is needed.	Go to Step 3.
STEP 2	Is the decision illegal, unethical, immoral, or alienating a population or demographic your organization serves?	
2a	Yes, there is an objective reason the decision should not be made.	Great catch, and speak up immediately! It's something that might have been overlooked by those involved in the decision prior to you. Stop the action, and call out the issue.
2b	No, I have no objections that fit these criteria.	Go to Step 3.
STEP 3	Do you understand the role you are expected to play in working toward the solution? Recall that these roles include decision-makers, the people who can say yes or no to high-level strategies and changes; consultants, those who offer options and their associated risks; and a Good Person to Be Informed, which describes most of the people in an organization.	
3a	Yes, I understand the role ! am expected to play, regardless of whether it's the role I prefer.	Go to Step 4.
3b	No, I'm unclear about my intended role in this situation.	Seek clarity from your leaders or team. Most people unsure of their role at this point will be a Good Person to Be Informed, but remember that this role is not passive, and it doesn't mean you can't offer feedback for what happens at your organization. All three roles have equal value within the organization.

continued

		You may even ask, "Are you asking me to be a consultant in how to address this issue?" If you're wondering, *Am I the decision-maker here?* you most likely aren't, as decision-makers typically know they are decision-makers. Settle into your role given the situation, and go to Step 4. *I thought to myself, "Am I the decision-maker here?" Asking this essentially answered the question for me. To add insult to injury, the social media account we were discussing in the meeting was our founder's profile—not to mention the money going into the campaign was hers as well. Needless to say, I wasn't the decision-maker.* *This left the two possible roles of being a consultant or a Good Person to Be Informed. I realized at this point I wasn't sure which one I was being asked to play. I jotted this down as the first question I would clarify when appropriate when returning to the meeting. This became next right action.* *At the meeting, I asked, "I know I may seem a little slow to catch up today, but are you asking me to consult and offer a few ideas to achieve your goal, or have you already decided, and I am to be informed?"* *Our founder answered in the meeting that she needed me to consult and offer ideas for her to make a decision on how to achieve her goal of properly shielding the brand on social media platforms.*

STEP 4	Are you struggling to buy into the strategy, decision, or change, or are you still struggling to settle into your role and use your expertise to take next right action toward the organization's goals?	
4a	Yes, I am not fully on board with the organization's decision or the role they are expecting me to play.	Go to Step 5. *I am not a fan of this strategy change because what we are doing is working. My preference, if I was the decision-maker, would be to continue executing as we are with all this momentum.*
4b	No, I understand the organization's strategy and the role I'm needed to play.	Go to Step 6.
STEP 5	Do you see specific risks with the decision or strategy that are based on your expertise rather than your opinion? In general, expertise is most helpful and considers how something could work, while opinions focus on why it won't work. Consider the differences that follow before proceeding.	
	OPINION Not relying on factual evidence or specialized knowledge Focused on personal preferences or beliefs Based solely on gut feelings, anecdotes, or speculation Reluctance to change because skill sets haven't been consistently updated Often includes conscious or unconscious biases Personal judgments, projections, or false interpretations Assumptions about or assignments of motive	**EXPERTISE** Based on data, research, evidence, policies, precedence, legislation, proven methodologies, case studies, and success stories Comes from training, education, or hands-on knowledge in specific areas Focused on what helps the potential of the business or organization Tends to capitalize on change by updating skill sets to help maintain readiness for what's next Includes input with heightened awareness of conscious or unconscious biases Information gathered and synthesized from experts, practitioners, and stakeholders Fact-based, observable behaviors and giving the benefit of doubt to others

continued

5a	No, my concerns aren't based in expertise. The decision simply isn't my preference.	Remember that while personal opinions can reflect valid concerns, they tend to focus on "why we can't" rather than "how we could." Jot down these opinions, and translate them into expertise-based input to be addressed when determining next right action. Once you've filtered out and set aside personal opinions, go to Step 6. *While there was some expertise in my head regarding the metrics from social media, I did have focus on my personal preferences or beliefs instead of our founder's idea of highest potential for the business. I had some judgments and assignments of motive that were fogging up my expertise that were exposed upon reflecting on Step 5.*
5b	Yes, I see a list of the risks with this decision, change, or unpreferred reality that are based in expertise.	Document those concerns now, and go to Step 6. *Now, back centered on bringing expertise to the situation, I documented a handful of my concerns given the strategy chosen. Some examples included notifying fans who consumed our weekly content on social media and deciding what to do with already-posted content on platforms.*
STEP 6	Do you feel ready to align your efforts with your role and the organization's goal?	
6a	Yes, I am aligned with the organization's overarching goals and ready to provide my input and energy toward the solution.	Go to Step 7. *At this point, I realized that the goal was not mine to decide or change, but it was clear that I could still make an impact on the situation by working in a constructive manner to help the team steer clear of my concerns.* *I felt reengaged knowing that finding our next right actions soon, given these concerns, was going to ensure that this decision would be least disruptive to our followers and ultimately our business.*

6b	No, there is too much of a gap between my expectations and those of the organization, and I'm unwilling to buy into focusing on how I could contribute given the circumstances.	It might be time to consider transitioning off your team or outside the organization. The choice always lies with you about whether to stay in joy or leave in peace. Both are incredibly peaceful decisions, but trying to remain in the third option of staying and hating or resisting only sabotages your chances of contributing to organizational results while fueling personal discontent. Sitting in this third option is a stance that cannot be tolerated for both the success of the organization and for an individual's own long-term happiness.
STEP 7	You're ready for next right action! Even if you have concerns, risks, or potential issues to be considered in addressing the unpreferred reality or the organization's decision, your opportunity to convert those into constructive impacts on the solution will soon happen by completing the final step of The Call to Greatness Framework.	

As you can see, the Organizational Alignment and Buy-In Decision Table was essential in revealing my role for what the situation required given the unexpected decision. With my list of concerns close by, I could rest assured I was clear about my role and ready to buy into next right action. This situation required a deeper dive into each tool of The Call to Greatness Framework to release me from several snags that would previously have left me stuck. In the final chapter, you will see how to use the list of concerns documented with this tool to do good, to sharpen next right action, and to solve the problem.

If Everyone's Opinion Counts, We'll Finally Get Buy-In!

Leaders in a large regional hospital needed to update a monitoring system used to improve patient care and outcomes. This would represent a significant change for frontline staff, and leaders decided that the people closest to the work should be partners in decision-making if this was to go smoothly. They hoped that consulting their team first would mean increased buy-in, more commitment, and a higher likelihood of success in the transition to the new technology.

After identifying three potential systems, the leaders asked their employees to try out all three during a two-week period. For simplicity, we'll call them Options A, B, and C. At the end of the try-out period, the employees voted. The votes, to the dismay of the decision-makers, were equally split among the three systems.

The leaders realized whatever choice they made was likely to anger two-thirds of the employees using it. They'd be able to say, "See?! They asked for my opinion, and they went in a different direction. They don't value my input!"

Worried about resistance, the leaders discussed whether to put the project on hold but decided that would be detrimental to patients and the communities they served. A few days before the final decision, additional external influences came into play: Another reputable brand in the industry had launched a product that offered better predictive analytics, seamless system integration, and data-collection tools. It was state-of-the-art technology. To sweeten the deal, the company was offering lower prices and bulk discounts for early adopters. These new external decision-making factors were colliding to steer the choice in a new direction. Option D became the front-runner and the proverbial no-brainer for the path the organization should take to best serve their patients in the long term.

But the excitement about the possibilities of Option D dissipated as the leaders worried about their employees feeling betrayed. Since this option hadn't been in consideration during voting, resistance could be even stronger.

Even so, the leaders ultimately couldn't ignore the promise and potential of Option D and began working on a communication strategy to explain and clarify the decision of proceeding with it. They did everything by the book for stellar change communication, creating a clear why statement, offering concise data analysis on the reasoning for the final decision, and even producing an inspirational message about the wonderful ways this new system would benefit patients.

How did this situation play out?

Several organizations across the country adopted the Option D system and experienced cost savings, efficiencies, and breakthroughs. At this organization, however, the implementation went poorly. The employees had been asked for their opinions, and their leaders had seemingly disregarded them. Many of the employees were angry at leadership for ignoring their input and blamed them for making a poor decision.

This was a classic case of failing to accurately identify decision-making roles in moving toward the solution. A lack of clarity about roles meant no one really understood who were the decision-maker(s), the consultant(s), and those who were a Good Person to Be Informed. Too many cooks were brought into the kitchen, as they say. Once the decision was made, the various teams failed to buy in, move into next right action, and wholeheartedly execute. The organization suffered financially because of poor implementation and culturally because of employee resentment.

This example demonstrates how the Organizational Alignment and Buy-in Decision Table could have been a lifesaver for all involved. Had the hospital leadership facilitated conversations with the tool from the start, they could have avoided the implementation challenges entirely. By clearly defining that staff would serve as consultants rather than decision-makers, the leaders would have properly set expectations. They would have transparently communicated that while employee input was valuable for considering the strengths and weaknesses of the original options, leadership retained final decision-making authority, especially when compelling new information emerged.

The tool would have supported the leaders in establishing a clear communication framework explaining how input would be considered, preventing the feeling that opinions were solicited only to be discarded. With properly defined roles, the teams would have understood their important contribution to the process while recognizing the reasons for selecting Option D in the end, ultimately leading to a higher likelihood of buy-in, a smoother transition to next right action and implementation, and improved patient outcomes—the very goal everyone shared from the beginning. Most important, the Decision Table would have facilitated the shift of energy, efforts, and focus from predecision role clarification to postdecision buy-in and execution.

Why Role Confusion Created Double Trouble

If it isn't clear by now, when you operate outside of your role, you create twin burdens: wasted energy and missed opportunity.

Several years back, my speaking engagements increased to several times per week, with travel to multiple cities in rapid succession. As these opportunities grew, our organization adjusted our staffing to provide appropriate administrative support for a speaker whose business was taking off.

My role transitioned from simply fulfilling speaking opportunities to a greater responsibility involving presenting on larger stages, creating new content, and writing a book on behalf of the company. Our founder asked me to prioritize these critical tasks while focusing additional time on staying connected with my growing client list to support them in implementing our leadership programs.

To enable this shift, I would receive increased administrative support from a colleague to handle tasks that had been consuming my time—booking travel, finding hotels, arranging rental cars, and managing logistics. While I should have embraced this change with enthusiasm for the time it would free up to focus on my new priorities, I struggled to understand my role in this transition.

This confusion doubled my suffering. I was covertly resisting because I loved the busyness of booking my travel, blocking off Fridays for this task. The complexity of coordinating different cities and timing could take several hours, but checking off numerous travel arrangements made me feel productive. It felt like an invigorating game of Tetris! However, these three to five hours could have been used for writing, strategic thinking, or deepening client relationships—the very tasks I had been asked to now prioritize by my leader! My attachment to my preferred approaches of the past led me to believe I wouldn't get as much done, but I wasn't accomplishing the right tasks for the potential of the business because I remained in the wrong role.

As the transition unfolded and my attachment to my old role dissolved, I eventually noticed a breakthrough. Clients would ask when I needed to leave for the airport toward the end of a speaking engagement, and my response was, "Honestly, I don't know."

While that may sound irresponsible and anxiety inducing to most, the reality is that I am not the decision-maker for that question.

My sole responsibility is to follow a process that our organization has created as a best practice that requires me to open my phone shortly after leaving the stage and follow the calendar my colleague has prepared. I check my schedule, which tells me where to go, what airport, and what terminal. I'm simply a Good Person to Be

Informed, and my response in my head is *I'm doin' it*. I follow the simple instructions in front of me.

This system allows me to recapture time, conserve energy, and fully trust my colleagues in their roles. At the same time, my administrative support person feels fully empowered and accountable for the actions and decisions she makes. Occasionally, although I should know better, I still feel compelled to intervene and question a particular choice made regarding my travel. Each time I step out of my lane, I find myself rusty after five years away from these tasks. I end up wasting valuable time, only to realize my colleague made the best decision based on available information.

A recent example drove this lesson home. During a trip to the San Bernardino, California, area, I noticed the chosen airport seemed farther away than flying into Los Angeles. Feeling a little frustrated with my colleague and thinking I could add value, I jumped in and booked a different flight. When I connected with my colleague to share the reasoning for my fix, I learned that a contractual requirement specified flying into the smaller county airport. My intervention forced her to rework everything at increased cost to our business while also ending up with a more inconvenient flight that landed late at night.

This was eye-opening because I had momentarily directed my annoyance at my colleague as if she was the decision-maker in this situation, only to find out the *real* decision-maker was the contractual obligation and the client's policies. She was a Good Person to Be Informed on this particular situation as well!

The consequences of my role confusion and subsequent next wrong action were noticeable and a double-negative: I wasted time that kept me from contributing to hitting my book deadline, and I thought I was helping but instead created rework because I didn't trust my colleague's expertise.

By surrendering control of tasks outside my role, I've gained back those precious Friday hours—time I now spend on higher-value work or at home enjoying quality time with my children. What once seemed like giving up control has become a form of freedom. Understanding and committing to your proper role aren't restrictive—they're liberating.

Two Uncomfortable Truths This Tool Can Reveal

Two difficult truths often bubble to the surface as teams complete the Organizational Alignment and Buy-in Decision Table. First, it can reveal employees who are unwilling to accept their role for what the situation is requiring. Second, it can reveal when an employee doesn't agree with the organization's current goals, changes, or strategies. Either of these situations is likely to cause immense suffering for the team member and conflict within a team.

The reality may be that people are unhappy that the organization is going in a direction that doesn't fit their preference. They aren't pleased with the changes, decisions, or new goals that have been chosen. They try to muscle their way into roles that they haven't been asked to play, or they long for the "good old days," when they could weigh in on all decisions. They choose personal preference over organizational potential.

I saw this situation happening at a small East Coast bank during a training I conducted. The bank was at a tough crossroads. The CEO had been hired to execute a bold new strategy of growth and modernization. The new CEO anticipated that, as with all changes involving significant goals and requirements, there would be natural resistance to the new direction. However, what he discovered instead was a burgeoning clash between two organizational identities. On one side stood the vision of regional expansion that featured updated technology and modern banking processes. On the other side was the cherished culture of a small personal local bank that had been the source of their previous success.

While most team members were leaning in to the exciting new path ahead, several had chosen a stance of digging their heels in and even accusing the executives of bringing in their "big bankism" to ruin the community-based spirit the bank was founded on. These mindsets were compounding into a steady supply of grumblings about "why they shouldn't have to" align with the new goals.

Although the CEO had extensive experience in navigating the natural resistance that accompanies change of this sort, he wondered whether the Organizational Alignment and Buy-In Decision Table could help his leadership team better empathize with employees who were processing the new requirements being asked of them while not lowering the standards of what the organization required moving forward. In other words, he wanted his leaders equipped with a tool to love teams up without forgetting to call them up to greatness and clarify where they are needed to contribute.

As his team began using the Decision Table and facilitated conversations with it in the branches where resistance was particularly high, he discovered that many employees simply did not want to work for a large bank focused on growth and rapid modernization. They preferred the culture and personal touch of a small local bank, which contrasted with the new vision that aimed to expand regionally.

In these cases, the leaders were able to invite people to complete the Organizational Alignment and Buy-in Decision Table, which essentially revealed two meaningful options moving forward:

1. Stay in joy, and fully contribute. Embrace the new direction, bring your expertise to navigate concerns along the way, and buy in to help make it happen.

2. Leave in peace. Recognize that this new path isn't aligned with your personal preferences or professional goals or values, and choose to find a more suitable opportunity where you can fully buy in.

The critical breakthrough is that both of these options revealed by the tool are *incredibly* peaceful and great options for all involved.

However, the third option of staying while constantly resisting, critiquing, or undermining the new direction and refusing to follow new processes is not helpful and would no longer be tolerated.

What made this approach powerful was its combination of compassion and clarity. It helped leaders support without enabling and clarify reality so employees could make better decisions. The leadership team didn't just show people the door; they offered them genuine support. For those choosing the option to leave in peace, they provided support in finding positions at other local banks that might better match their career aspirations.

A bonus to using the tool was the transformation in their confidence in addressing misalignment to the strategy. What once was a potentially difficult discussion about buy-in to roles, which leaders avoided in fear that it could get confrontational, was now able to be conversational and clear, thanks to the Organizational Alignment and Buy-in Decision Table.

WATCH FOR CONFUSING THE WHAT WITH THE HOW

The higher up you are in organizational leadership, the more time you should be spending clarifying goals and supporting people in knowing their roles. If you're doing this well as a high-level leader, you should not have to get bogged down in procedures *at all*. In fact, directors-and-above positions may spend 80 percent of their time repeating and clarifying goals (or "what we are doing") and the roles people are being asked to play. This leaves the departmental execution and accountability for working toward those organizational goals (or the "how to do it") to those who are paid to do so.

That said, I often see another flavor of role confusion in organizations, in which people start confusing the responsibility of the what, which refers to setting strategy and direction, with the accountability of the how, which are the actions taken to execute those business goals.

An executive team I consulted with at one of the largest US insurance companies was experiencing what turned out to be this phenomenon during a transformation initiative they were going through. The CEO believed he had communicated the new goals and strategies clearly, consistently, and in every venue possible. But in our training sessions, a lingering state of resistance and confusion remained, and we couldn't quite put a finger on the cause.

In an effort to come at the issue from a different angle, we provided a printout of the Organizational Alignment and Buy-in Decision Table and had each executive run through it as a self-reflection exercise. Unexpectedly, in the process of completing the tool, a team member popped his head up and began sharing his thoughts: "Fine. If this is really where the organization is headed and what needs to be executed, we're going to need some guidance or a playbook as to how to get it done! We'll need some clear directions on *how* to do it." Many others echoed in agreement.

The tool had gently poked at the blockage we'd been dancing around and helped the CEO pinpoint the true problem.

His main responsibility was to set and communicate the strategy, clarifying what needed to be done, outlining the goals, and refining the roles of the group. He was in charge of what needed to be done. His executive team, on the other hand, was responsible for how it got executed. In other words, the how is what they were accountable for and, frankly, paid good money for. They had the freedom, within a handful of set business constraints, to establish their departmental plans, approaches, and procedures to deliver on that vision.

In this case, however, they seemed to be trying to offload the bulk of the how back onto the CEO in order to deliver on the new goals set. This conversation also exposed that some of the executives were frustrated that they didn't have the ability to change the goals and even the roles they were being asked to play in the situation. They had been burning calories trying to influence a decision that was already made when their *true* decision-making influence was in establishing and executing the procedures—the how—to reach those goals from their part of the organization.

This seemingly minor breakthrough allowed the executive team to acknowledge what had been months of underlying conflict and stagnation that had halted the group from moving into next right action with their teams. Each executive committed to return in the next few weeks with a high-level plan based on their expertise in their area of the business as to how they saw their teams delivering on the new goals set by the CEO. The fight for what needed to be done had finally come to rest, and all energy and focus were freed up for next right action.

FINAL WORDS OF WISDOM IN COMPLETING THIS STEP

In the stories throughout this chapter, you've learned about several teams that found clarity and greatly reduced conflict through the Organizational Alignment and Buy-In Decision Table. The reflections you're inviting through this step of The Call to Greatness Framework aren't always easy on the ego, especially if someone is learning they are being asked to play a different role from the one they thought they had in the situation. For this reason, it is helpful to follow a few final tips to get the most out of the tool and to overview common situations in which you'll most likely need to use it.

Here is a list of what to keep in mind when using the Organizational Alignment and Buy-in Decision Table:

- Start with love when using this tool. Have you established a good relationship with the person or team with whom you are using this tool?
- As a leader, settle into your own role by reflecting on the Decision Table before using it with your teams. If a leader isn't aligned, their team might have challenges with alignment and buy-in as well. Here's a general rule: **Where the leader goes, so goes the team.**
- Keep the tool visual as much as possible. Print out the Organizational Alignment and Buy-In Decision Table from this book, and give each person a copy or share the tool virtually as you facilitate reflection. Another effective approach is sitting side by side with people while looking at the tool in front of you on the table or desk. This positioning feels as if you are on the same team, completing an exercise instead of the team member being coached into a role. Asking the questions out loud and directly to a team member, without the tool's visual representation, can ignite the ego and resistance.
- Remind people often that during their careers, they will likely play all three of the roles at different times. They are not losing their ability to make decisions or be consulted. Rather, they are ensuring that they aren't spending excess energy trying to contribute in the wrong role for what the situation is requiring of them.

COMMON SITUATIONS FOR APPLYING THE DECISION TABLE

The following are some situations or individuals you may encounter when implementing the Organizational Alignment and Buy-In Table:

- Employees who want to set (or push back on) company goals or strategies that have already been decided by the board of directors, CEO, or senior leaders
- Complaints or questions about why employees weren't consulted about a decision (e.g., "Why didn't they ask the people closest to the work about this?")
- Employees who try to "fix" strategies they don't like or who require new skills or knowledge (e.g., "Why can't we do it the way we've always done it?")
- People who insist that their personal preferences should trump the business potential of decisions, strategies, and standardized work processes

Now that you have helped your team clean up thinking, take accountability for their part, and know their roles in the solution, the stage is set to surge into next right action. However, just because people seem clear on what to do next to contribute doesn't mean that lingering fear, doubt, or old narratives won't quietly creep back into their minds and resurface those limiting beliefs of "why we can't."

The next section shows you exactly how and why this happens and gives you the necessary tools to move beyond it when it does.

PART III

ANSWER THE CALL

Are you feeling a bit of momentum now?

With role clarity now spoken for, your team is on the verge of confidently stepping into next right action.

The newfound clarity gained from completing Steps 1 through 4 of The Call to Greatness Framework makes the path ahead visible. Now it is time to innovate and execute given your unique circumstances. Innovation here isn't always about revolutionary breakthroughs (although that can happen!) or waiting for perfect conditions; it's about finding the right move forward that actually works given the reality you're facing. Execution is the follow-through, committing to action rather than remaining stuck in analysis.

However, even so, a lingering fog of "why we can't" can persist in the minds of your team that halts them from forging ahead.

So why might someone who is clear on the problem, is accountable for their part in the situation thus far, and knows their role in the solution still struggle to move into next right action?

The root cause of this inaction is familiar to all of us, is rooted deep in our human wiring, and can be simplified to one word: fear. It's that simple.

Whether it's fear of failure, fear of choosing the wrong path among many options, fear of repercussions, fear of loss, or even fear of success itself, the feeling of fear is not caused necessarily by what happens to us; it is the story we believe about what is going to happen to us. It helps to remember *fear* as **F**alse **E**vents **A**ppearing **R**eal. It is more the story about what *may* happen, not the reality of what *is* happening that scares us. Once people become fearful about what could happen ahead, they resort to overthinking, catastrophizing, or doubling down on why they can't proceed.

When overthinking becomes persistent, the mind finds all the internal or external barriers in the way of moving forward. When you are overthinking, you are actually not trying to decide what to do. Often, you are trying to decide how to eliminate the consequences or the risk. While it's wise to consider the potential dangers ahead in any choice you make, true wisdom comes from knowing that no decision is without them. If you or a business only made decisions without risks, you'd make no decisions, and this is precisely what gets people frozen in inaction.

In the worst cases, this habit spirals into resistance to change, analysis paralysis, or procrastination. Instead of these barriers becoming normalized considerations to navigate during next right action, they become the reasons people can't succeed instead of the unpreferred reality in which they must.

The three next right action tools at your disposal to complete this final step of The Call to Greatness Framework are all versatile, but it's important to understand that each one shines and thrives better in certain situations. In other words, each tool has its inherent strengths to nudge people over the finish line and ensure that they take next right action.

ADVANCED TECHNIQUE—THE SKIP TO NEXT RIGHT ACTION

Every unpreferred reality is best run through the entire Call to Greatness Framework. This will increase the likelihood of most effectively loving someone up and calling them up to greatness and next right action. However, with experience and repetitions of coaching people through the framework, you can develop a sense (almost like a radar) for how tolerant or capable someone may be to skip directly to next right action. High-performing teams that are well-versed and fluent in the tools of the framework often use this to their benefit and as a competitive advantage to quickly shift to next right action. In other words, they maintain a steady practice of keeping good hygiene with their thinking, they quickly find their

continued

part in issues, and they can shape-shift nearly immediately into the correct role for what the situation merits. With very little friction that comes up in each of those steps for their teams, the focus channels nearly immediately to the selection of the next right action tool. However, each time this is done, it runs the risk of skimming the top of the situation and failing to extract the *best* next actions to address the unpreferred reality.

With that in mind, I've outlined each tool at a thirty-thousand-foot view to aid in narrowing down your selection of how to best finish the call to greatness based on where the person or team seems to be stuck.

If it is your first time going through the book, I recommend reading Part III all the way through, as you would a normal book. However, once you have learned each tool, moving forward, you can skip to the chapter with the tool you need for the situation.

CALL TO GREATNESS STEP 5. TAKE NEXT RIGHT ACTION

Your Three Tools for Next Right Action (and When It's Best to Use Them)

1. SITUATION, BACKGROUND, ASSESSMENT, AND RECOMMENDATIONS (SBAR) TOOL

When moving fully into next right action, the first tool that most people turn to is the Situation, Background, Assessment, and Recommendations (SBAR) tool.

This tool creates a high-level overview of the unpreferred reality you have been addressing and directs anyone completing it to begin documenting their initial recommendations to start solving the issue. This tool is highly useful, especially if next right action is somewhat straightforward and obvious. Think of this as your all-purpose Swiss army knife tool to direct any conversation toward possible next right actions.

2. THINKING INSIDE THE BOX TOOL

The second tool is the Thinking Inside the Box tool. This is particularly effective for moving toward a goal given the constraints, circumstances, excuses, or competing priorities that seem to be in the way.

Use this tool when your team is stuck, experiencing barriers, overwhelmed by competing priorities, or tempted to blame external forces for why they can't move toward their goals. It helps focus energy and conversations on what can be done, right now, within the current unpreferred reality they are facing.

3. NEGATIVE BRAINSTORMING TOOL

The Negative Brainstorming tool is ideal for progressing despite fears of what lies ahead, concerns about how to accomplish the task, or resistance to change or decisions.

This tool is effective when you are getting ready for an upcoming change and your team is expressing fears, concerns, or worries. The tool is also useful if your group is dealing with a challenge that has essentially already been decided and it is your job to find next right action and make it as least disruptive as possible to your organization.

Now that you have an idea of where each next right action tool is most effective, it is time to make your selection to complete The Call to Greatness Framework and ensure that your team takes next right action.

If you find yourself still unsure or one of the barriers listed doesn't seem to fit what may be happening, simply continue reading and begin with the SBAR tool as your starting point to narrowing down next right action. If, after completing the SBAR tool, you aren't feeling clear enough on what action to take, continue taking the situation through the remaining two next right action tools.

Finally, if you feel you selected the wrong tool and haven't made progress toward next right action, simply pick another tool and complete it. Remember, any action steps taken after completing the entire Call to Greatness Framework won't be wasted steps because of the new information you'll discover from operating out of that clarity.

Once you hit the new unpreferred reality or place of confusion, begin the steps of The Call to Greatness Framework again with the new information and insights you've acquired.

CHAPTER 5

THE SITUATION, BACKGROUND, ASSESSMENT, AND RECOMMENDATIONS (SBAR) TOOL

Now that you have an outline of all three RBL tools available for moving through the final step of the call to greatness, it's time to ensure that all the great reflection done thus far turns into action. One of the easiest ways to do that is with the SBAR tool.

SBAR gives you a structure for getting out of your head and moving your insights from reflection into reality. It's a straightforward way to quickly frame the issue and then capture any first ideas for next right action, even if you're still sorting through some uncertainty.

Completing the tool ensures that people stop hiding out behind problem identification and lean fully into problem-solving. It's a simple way to summarize the issue and open the door to collaboration if needed, without slipping back into venting, spinning, or hesitation.

A bonus is that using the tool saves time because leaders aren't solving, directing, managing, explaining, and jumping in to fix the problems brought to them. They can stop overmanaging and underleading. Doing this reinforces a limiting belief that people are incapable of or incompetent at solving problems. By overmanaging and taking next right action for people because it is "quicker for me to do it," leaders create an incentive to return to the leader the next time they have a challenge.

Let's first overview the tool and then cover a few practical examples of how leaders and teams used the SBAR tool to spot key issues or opportunities in their business and not only propose creative solutions but actually follow through on them to drive real results.

HOW THE SBAR TOOL WORKS

The SBAR tool starts with making the issue visible. All you need is a pen, a piece of paper, and a simple template designed to spur self-reflection and clarification of the issue. (Remember that the ego loves verbal dialogue and ambiguity. For this reason, the SBAR tool, especially when you first begin using it, *must* be written and visual.)

After validating the feelings or experience of an unpreferred reality, the employee is asked to address four areas:

Situation (What is the current situation, issue, or unpreferred reality?)

This must be one sentence. Any good writer will tell you that it's easier to write long than to write succinctly. Condensing the issue to one simple sentence is essential to this exercise. This will require thinking deeply about the crux of the issue and getting intentional through self-reflection. Brevity also simmers down the ego's impulse to vent, judge, or create a story. Notice that the Edit Your Story tool is naturally integrated into this step.

Background (What is the *relevant* background? Why are you bringing this up?)

Background must be current, relevant, and connected to organizational strategies, key initiatives, or goals. This helps people see where they are spending time and resources on things the organization isn't focused on. This provides context and history, but not information from an unofficial company historian (i.e., "Before trying to solve this issue, we must first go back to 1979, prior to the internet and two court cases ago . . .").

Assessment (What expertise, *not opinions*, have you tapped into?)

This section should include the most detailed information. A favorite RBL mantra is that "expertise is far more valuable than opinion." Write about relevant facts, the science and data, best practices, proven methodologies and effective processes, legal precedence, and evidence. Assessment also could include people who have been consulted, analytics, company policy, established procedures, case studies, etc.

Opinions, which are unfounded gut feelings or personal preferences and often include conscious or unconscious biases, judgments, and assignments of motive, should not make the cut for this section. (You may notice that the most opinionated people often have the least expertise. Refer to the Organizational Alignment and Buy-In Decision Table for help identifying opinions versus expertise.)

Recommendations (What ideas can they offer for progress toward resolving the issue or achieving the goal? What resources or trade-offs must be considered?)

We discourage suggesting only one solution, because typically that will be based on preference or what someone is comfortable doing rather

continued

than what is best for the organization. The ego loves to offer "the way you *must* do this" or insists on "my way." Employees should be encouraged to identify *at least* two potential right actions, and preferably more. Potential solutions should factor in the costs, benefits, and trade-offs. Multiple possible recommendations of next right action encourage mental flexibility and creativity and demonstrate a willingness to see the situation from many perspectives. Several suggestions demonstrate willingness to buy into an option the team can get the most agreement on. The attitude shifts from personal preference to team potential.

FINAL STEP—Ask for Commitments

From the clean thinking and problem clarification enabled by the SBAR tool, the employee and leader agree on the best recommendation(s) to act on and finish with a commitment from the person who completed the SBAR, detailing what actions they need to take and a timeframe for when they need to complete those actions. This becomes an easy follow-up conversation starter to check on progress. Simply ask, "What did you commit to the last time we connected?"

If an SBAR tool doesn't end with who, doing what, and by when, then it is as if it *never* happened.

Digital Toolkit: Want to download your own SBAR template and tutorial video to use with your team? Follow the QR code below to do so. You can also download the full Call to Greatness Framework Toolkit from the same link.

Once the employee has completed the SBAR tool in writing, it sets up a development conversation based on thought partnership as opposed to a leader-to-employee coaching dynamic. The leader listens closely and ensures that the model's simple framework has been followed.

The SBAR template helps conversations move from ambiguity to clarity. It facilitates clean thinking, a clear view of the problem, and, most important, possible next right actions to be taken. Used consistently, the SBAR tool helps leaders maintain boundaries with their teams, weaning them off the temptation to overmanage and underlead.

I often say, "The person who takes the time to mentally process the problem is the one who takes action on it." This couldn't be truer with the SBAR tool, because the person who has the issue and completes the tool is responsible for the identified action steps. More important, the person creating the SBAR understands that their input has added value in the space between an unpreferred reality and the ideal future. The SBAR creates a win-win interaction—the employee is empowered to act, and the leader ensures that the person with the issue doesn't dump it on someone else.

The SBAR cuts through ambiguity faster than any RBL tool that we have. It is the fast track for capturing a summary of the work done thus far in The Call to Greatness Framework and revealing next right action. It can have big impact, and we've seen it have a big impact in organizations in all the industries where we work. Let's look at a few examples.

THE FULL CALL TO GREATNESS IN ACTION—VIRAL ON TIKTOK

In addressing the strategic decision to modify RBL's social media approach with The Call to Greatness Framework so far, I had cleaned up my thinking, simmered down a bit, seen my part in the situation, and recognized what I could do differently moving forward to avoid getting caught in this trap again. Now I knew my role as a consultant.

It was time for choosing our next right action, but what tool did we need to best do so?

Thinking it would be best to outline the problem and begin collecting our scattered thoughts at a high level, we selected the SBAR tool. Additionally, we hadn't yet heard of any constraints set in place by our founder as we began our brainstorm of ideas, which ruled out Thinking Inside the Box for the time being.

Over the next few days, my colleagues and I rehashed the situation and the relevant background, conducted some analysis, and then offered recommendations on how we could proceed to achieve our founder's goal.

The SBAR we came up with follows.

Situation

Our founder's leadership clips went viral on TikTok, generating both excitement and a high volume of negative and out-of-context comments.

Background

A core part of our business strategy is ensuring that our content is on message and provides modern low-drama leadership tips and techniques. It is critical that it is delivered with quality and consistency. We aim for new audiences to encounter our ideas in a way that represents our philosophy's distinct spirit and impact. Viral visibility is exciting, but if not managed well, it can dilute or misrepresent our brand.

Analysis

We reviewed the insights from the videos:

- Approximately 35 percent of the comments were critical or misinterpreted the message.
- About 40 percent of incoming speaking inquiries from the viral videos were low-quality leads (i.e., not aligned with our target audience).
- These leads were taking time from best serving our current clients.
- An estimated 70 percent of viewers encountering the content were hearing our philosophy for the first time, often reacting without the broader context of our full approach to leadership and coaching people in a loving way when they are stuck in drama.

While the exposure increased brand visibility, it also carried reputational risk if first impressions were based on isolated or misunderstood soundbites.

Recommendations

To move forward, we generated several next-step options, each with potential costs and benefits.

1. **Continue with our current social media strategy (aka, take no action).**
   - Cost: Risk of more misinterpretation and possible long-term brand erosion
   - Benefit: Maximizing reach while momentum is high and continuing to attract more viewers
2. **Create longer-form video content for TikTok.**
   - Cost: Lower chance of virality compared with short clips

continued

- Benefit: More opportunity to provide fuller context and educate new viewers properly

3. **Comment on viral videos to reframe discussions.**
   - Cost: Labor-intensive and may invite further debate
   - Benefit: Actively guide new audience members toward deeper understanding and more resources
4. **Shift content focus back to channels where fans have already been exposed to our speakers (e.g., our newsletter and podcast).**
   - Cost: May slow short-term audience growth and will lose momentum of current viral videos
   - Benefit: Ensures we are engaging followers where they are familiar with our speakers and can hear full sessions or longer stories around the viral topics

By using The Call to Greatness Framework and ultimately the SBAR tool for offering possible action steps for our founder, the internal team and I were able to quickly get regrounded in facts rather than opinions and properly fulfill the role of consultant in the situation.

With a clear SBAR in front of her, our founder was able to make a decisive choice for the business that avoided the possibility of getting pulled into defensiveness or arguments online while supporting our fans old and new with the content they love.

Fixing the Habit of Fixing—From Doer to Leader

An example of the "let me fix it for you" leadership pattern is Chris, a high performer who was promoted to leadership in a highly innovative large pharmaceutical company. Chris was committed to proving himself and building credibility with his team. He worked hard to build trust, show competence as a leader, and support team members.

Chris had been taught that good leadership meant never asking the team to do something he wasn't willing to do himself. He jumped in to solve problems, so team members knew he had their backs. He established an open-door policy to facilitate communication and to remain approachable.

Using this textbook version of good leadership, Chris became aware that the more he "helped" people, the more they asked for his help. He'd often take next right action for them because deep down, he enjoyed the feeling of adding value by doing some of the old tasks he used to do previously.

Over time, team members became dependent on his expertise for the simplest tasks. He spent so much time solving low-risk issues and putting out fires that his days became long and exhausting. He'd run hard and fast all day, tackling problems, and by the end of the week, his own to-do list would be twice as long as when the week started.

This also meant he was pulled away from the strategic planning his role required. He began feeling resentful when people popped into his office to say, "Hey, do you have a minute?" He was overwhelmed and could feel resentment toward his team bubbling up.

During a coaching session with us, Chris talked about an employee, Denise, who had approached him for a "got-a-minute?" meeting. She was irritated about a technology conversion that had been scheduled over a weekend. It hadn't gone smoothly. Her story to Chris went like this:

> *Did you hear what happened with the conversion over the weekend? Our team did our part, but IT totally dropped the ball and was a complete disaster! They misjudged the resources, support, and help they'd need to pull this off. After talking to a few people*

in the break room, it sounds like it's going to be days until we even know where this serious lack of competence has landed us. I bet we won't be able to adequately support clients for weeks. They seriously can't manage their way out of a paper bag, and it is showing on this project.

After Chris shared the story with me, I offered to show him the SBAR, a tool that could help both Chris and Denise in this challenging situation.

Later, Chris used the SBAR with Denise instead of taking his typical approach of investigating or intervening with all the parties to solve the problem. He began by validating Denise's experience by saying, "I really appreciate you bringing this issue up. It's very disappointing that the conversion hasn't gone well, and I see that you're annoyed. I'd like to think through this situation a bit more intentionally with you if you are game. I think it may help us both find some clarity and a way forward." Denise expressed her willingness to give it a try. Sitting down with Denise, Chris took a notebook and began writing *S*, *B*, *A*, and *R* on the paper. This started the process of helping her question and reconsider the sense she was making of this experience.

After about five minutes of working through the tool together, Denise's story was clearer and more focused:

S*ituation: Our IT colleagues ran into a challenge on the data conversion over the weekend.*

B*ackground: This conversion is a top priority for our Transformation 2030 strategy, and this phase must be completed before the work can be handed off to the next phase.*

A*ssessment: I (Denise) am missing information as to the extent of the errors that are affecting the team. While the project timeline appears to be pushed back two weeks, I have a meeting scheduled tomorrow morning to learn more about what specifically happened* *to the data during the conversion. So far, only about 15 percent of our clients have been affected by the situation, and of those 15 percent, only a couple are key active users on the system.*

***R**ecommendations:*

1. *Stay in my own lane and wait for further updates from the IT team.*
2. *Connect with the IT experts to get more informed about what happened, collect data, and consider what would be most helpful for them as we communicate about progress.*
3. *Offer to help the team, even if it is to order in food or buy everyone a coffee because they have been working day and night to remedy the situation.*
4. *Reach out to the customer service team to explain the issue and consider possible solutions they have.*
5. *Create a quick presentation or communication plan to inform my team and potentially other departments so we can prevent unhelpful speculation and shut down gossip and speculation.*

After doing the SBAR, Denise had simmered down. Now that her thinking was clear, she adopted a more neutral tone as she talked. She realized she hadn't brought enough detailed analysis to the conversation, and in this situation, she also was stepping outside her lane. The SBAR tool made her see that being helpful, rather than judgmental, was a better way to serve the business and greatly influenced her five recommendations.

Her original story, long on blame and short on data, had shifted. The insight brought about a longer conversation with her leader about her patterns: jumping to conclusions, judging instead of helping, and moving into others' lanes at work. The tool inspired insights that helped Denise commit to using SBAR prior to coming to her colleagues to discuss problems as a way of pre-processing and cleaning up her thinking. This would keep her from simply complaining about frustrating situations and instead remind her to offer ideas to help. Denise finished with commitments to two of her recommendations.

Once people get into the habit of using the SBAR tool to self-reflect, clean up thinking, and pre-process a difficult issue, the conversation starts from a different place. Instead of seeing adversaries, people see thought partners to help them more quickly get to solutions and next right action.

Thought partnership about how to proceed creates continuous learning and knowledge transfer across the organization, as opposed to expecting someone else to jump in and fix the problem. Chris continued to work with Denise and his other team members. They used the SBAR tool, and it soon became the standard communication model. Chris broke the habit of jumping in to fix issues. In doing so, he empowered his team to use their expertise and freed time for himself to focus on more strategic planning and higher-level projects. Chris felt much less short on staff because the tool allowed him to fully use the talented staff he *already* had.

An Unexpected Innovation Unfolds from an SBAR

At a company I was consulting with that specializes in electrical building infrastructures, a new product line of electrical enclosures created unexpected challenges on the production floor. The packaging process, which was needed to protect the units during shipping, was struggling to keep up.

The unusual shape of the enclosures, combined with limitations on the existing packaging machinery, made it difficult to secure the products efficiently without increasing material costs or shipping volume. Left unsolved, the issue risked driving up operational costs, delaying shipments, and hurting overall profitability.

The team knew they needed a solution, but instead of immediately jumping to traditional process improvements, they used the SBAR tool to fully frame the problem and explore all options, including a breakthrough idea that would eventually come from an unexpected place.

***S**ituation: Shipping costs and packaging waste increased significantly after the launch of a new product line of electrical enclosures.*

***B**ackground: The company's operational strategy focuses on delivering high-quality, durable products while maintaining efficiency in logistics and sustainability efforts. Increased shipping costs not only cut into margins but also conflicted with the corporate commitment to waste reduction.*

Assessment:

- *Packaging costs per unit rose by 18 percent compared with projections.*
- *Shipping volume expanded because current packaging did not nest products efficiently, leading to higher freight costs.*
- *Internal teams had attempted minor redesigns but found little improvement because the product's shape (bulky and irregular) made traditional packing methods inefficient.*

***R**ecommendations: Through the SBAR reflection, the team shared some conventional ideas and eventually an unconventional next possible action:*

1. *Redesign internal packaging inserts to better stabilize products.*
    - *Cost: Minor investment in new insert tooling*
    - *Benefit: Potential to reduce damaged goods and better stackability*

2. *Negotiate with freight carriers for volume-based rate adjustments.*
   - *Cost: Administrative and negotiation time*
   - *Benefit: Lower per-unit shipping cost even if packaging improvements are modest*
3. *Pilot flat-pack shipping models in which minimal assembly is required by the customer.*
   - *Cost: Could require additional customer communication, inconvenience, and minor product adjustments*
   - *Benefit: Could dramatically reduce volume shipped, saving on freight and packaging costs*
4. *Partner with a consultant specializing in origami-based packaging design. (Chosen)*
   - *Cost: Consultant engagement fee and prototype development time*
   - *Benefit: High potential to dramatically reduce wasted space by using creative folds and techniques the current system is capable of programming that have not been considered by conventional packaging teams*

Without slowing down to apply SBAR and think beyond traditional fixes, the operations team might have stayed stuck trying to tweak an unsolvable problem.

By partnering with an origami expert, an unexpected but relevant outside perspective, the organization found an unlikely innovation that not only creatively worked around the issue but also led to significant cost savings all around.

An SBAR a Day Kept the Bottlenecks at Bay

At a global manufacturing company, the finance team had a problem that was quietly draining time, money, and trust: Credit approvals for dealer financing were taking far too long.

On paper, the process looked efficient. But in reality, it was lacking structure, which eventually created inefficiencies and bottlenecks.

Dealers would submit applications. Relationship managers would send them along. Decision-makers would review them and quickly realize they didn't have enough information to make a confident call on the approval. Was the financial history complete? Were there any strategic risks to this deal? What options had been considered before sending it up the chain?

Every time those answers were unclear, the decision-makers had to send questions back. Then more clarifications. Then another follow-up. A little phone tag mixed with a lot of pulling their hair out. You get the picture. Each round of rework stretched a decision that could have taken days into a process that took four to six weeks, sometimes costing the company's dealers critical sales opportunities.

The leadership team knew they didn't need a massive system overhaul. What they needed was a better way to structure the conversation itself.

That's when they introduced the SBAR tool as a way to streamline communication and hopefully arrive at next right action faster. Rather than informal, piecemeal submissions, every credit request now had to follow a clear structure:

- A short, clear statement of the situation
- Relevant background data with no fluff
- An objective analysis of risk and opportunity
- Clear recommendations for next steps

Instead of sending half-formed requests up the chain, the structure of the SBAR naturally embedded a layer of pre-processing at a deeper level. This allowed for a more complete report to be submitted that equipped the decision-maker with more information, which inevitably guided them straight to action.

The payoff of this tweak was almost immediate.

In conversations with decision-makers, they reported feeling 50 to 60 percent more confident making first-pass approvals without needing extra clarification. Rework and email chains shrank dramatically. And most important, time to decision dropped by ten to fourteen business days. That's two full weeks shaved off the approval process, without new technology, without more training sessions, and without micromanaging.

The breakthrough wasn't a fancy new workflow. It was a cultural commitment to a simple tool, shared accountability, and next right action.

By using the SBAR tool, the company's global finance team didn't just speed up approvals. They also protected millions of dollars in dealer sales pipelines and showed what's possible when better tools for thinking facilitate better business decisions.

Productive Feedback Minus Drama and Venting

In the same organization, a different part of the business used the SBAR in a different way to improve an idea-gathering process to find additional innovation and breakthroughs.

Leaders originally had solicited employees' ideas through a survey to improve work processes or suggest other enhancements that would improve the business. Within a few weeks, the organization had nearly five hundred submissions, but leaders quickly discovered that many of the ideas offered were shortsighted or, worse, consisted of paragraphs of venting and complaining about the way things currently were.

To change this unhelpful dynamic, the team in charge of the initiative added an SBAR requirement in the next phase of the submission process. They followed up on each submission, asking people to update their idea using the tool, hoping it would spark self-reflection and invite possible solutions to the issues as opposed to simply pointing out problems. After doing so, the submissions plummeted from five hundred to eighty.

Though the number of submissions dramatically dropped, the majority of the eighty remaining ideas were well thought-out, based on clean thinking and a clearly defined problem. The submissions were filled with practical ways the organization could improve work processes and eliminate inefficiencies. Furthermore, each idea was rooted in willingness to take action to further the organization's goals.

This added step acted as a natural boundary to ensure that people were considering possible next right actions instead of simply hiding out behind problem identification and spiraling into complaining. The tool simultaneously invited deeper reflection on next steps while ensuring that team members didn't feel shut down when offering necessary feedback.

What to Watch for with the SBAR Tool

After nearly a decade of both using the SBAR tool and teaching it to thousands of leaders, I've seen patterns to watch for that might sabotage your best efforts.

- Even after consistent use of the SBAR tool, the temptation might be to get back to talking through the situation rather than writing it down. Resist this temptation! This is the ego's attempt to avoid making the tool visual, which gives the SBAR much of its power. Remember that the ego's playground is verbal dialogue and ambiguity. Watch for, "I know you want me to write this down, but I'm an out-loud thinker. Sometimes I just need to spill the issue all out there, and *then* I'll clean it up later and move forward . . ."

- Be sure to adhere to the constraints baked into the directions of the tool (e.g., the situation is one sentence and the background is relevant to organizational strategies and goals). The SBAR should be concise and relatively short, not several pages.
- Some conversations may require multiple SBARs because smaller connected issues may come up. If a new issue comes up as you are discussing a different SBAR, simply begin a new one and write out the situation in one sentence to capture it. Then, gently return to the original SBAR you were working on and see it through to the finish. From there, you can shift attention to the second SBAR. Sometimes one anchoring SBAR will reveal other layers of the issue that need addressing. In my own life, I think of this as similar to the situation in which all three of my little kiddos are crying at the same time. My current skill set as a father allows me to take care of only one at a time (although, somehow, my wife is capable of taking care of all three at once!). What I do is acknowledge that each one is struggling (this is metaphorically beginning an SBAR on their issue) so they feel heard. Then I return to the first child with the most pressing need to get started. Once taken care of, I move to the next.
- Avoid using the SBAR tool for manipulation. It's not designed to tell people *what* to think but to help shape *how* they are thinking about a challenging work situation and what next right action could be. It brings the best of people's expertise forward given their diverse backgrounds and encourages dialogue.

- The SBAR isn't intended to solve every complex problem your team is facing. Many organizations have advanced systems, algorithms, or software to make deeply nuanced decisions. The tool is mainly designed to dislodge people out of "why we can't" thinking and tap into creativity, innovation, and collaboration. Often, the SBAR tool will point to obvious internal decision-making tools that aren't being used to their fullest, or it will remind you to dust off available resources that might be underused within the team or organization.

The SBAR tool is also the best tool selection if you are sensing that your team or someone is—

- Needing fast, high-level problem solving
  - Seeking their first ideas for next right action
  - Wanting a way to summarize an issue and collaborate with others on recommendations to solve it in the short term, midterm, and long term
- Hiding out behind problem identification and not moving to problem-solving
  - Still caught in complaining or venting about the issue
  - Spinning in their thoughts or offering too much detail about an issue
  - Known for bringing up too many issues at once
  - Taking a long time to get to the point of the conversation
  - Often beginning with, "Hey, do you have a minute?" and needs twenty to forty-five minutes
- Lacking confidence
  - Knowing what to do but constantly seeking approval or permission

    - Needing a second set of eyes to think through an issue
    - Lacking confidence that what they say or do will add value
    - Fearing failure or making a wrong decision that their leader wouldn't approve of
- Struggling to take accountability for their role in the situation
    - Trying to have you jump in and fix the issue for them
    - Dropping unprocessed and messy work on others to fix or figure out

In our work among countless organizations, many leaders have reported that the SBAR tool alone was able to elevate their teams' impact, efficiency, and professionalism at all levels. As leaders consistently invite employees to use the tool, they lean into problem-solving from consistent clear thinking and discover next right action more quickly. It is that powerful.

CHAPTER 6

THINKING INSIDE THE BOX TOOL

Another place where people get stuck even when next right action may seem obvious is when, after glancing at the work ahead, real or perceived barriers stand in the way of progress. It often sounds like, "We'd love to move forward, but we'd need X, Y, or Z taken care of first" or perhaps "I hear what you are saying, but you don't quite understand our competing priorities or the complex challenges involved in getting there."

As these barriers accumulate, a paralysis can set in. The mind becomes so crowded with roadblocks and extenuating circumstances that the path forward disappears entirely and next right action seems unfindable.

This moment of overwhelm signals the perfect opportunity to turn to the next RBL tool in The Call to Greatness Framework, called Thinking Inside the Box, to guide someone toward discovering their next possible steps given these barriers.

But wait a minute; isn't thinking *outside* the box the way to innovation and creative ideas when someone is stuck?

Proven Guilty, Thinking Outside the Box Is No Longer Innocent (or Helpful)

Conventional leadership wisdom has long glorified outside-the-box thinking as the key to innovative ideas.

Yet my experience reveals a startling and sometimes unpopular truth: **Asking teams to think outside the box leads to an argument with reality that you lose, but only 100 percent of the time.**

I learned this lesson the hard way during one of my first brainstorming sessions as a team leader. With enthusiasm, I invited my team to a huddle to think outside the box to find ideas for solving a persistent issue. A hand flew up, and a first suggestion came quickly: "I've got it! Let's hire five more people." It was a brilliant solution, except for the hiring freeze announced in my previous meeting that morning.

My response with that information churning in the back of my mind?

"Thank you," I said, "but actually, we can't. It's not possible at the moment."

Another colleague swooped in to one-up that idea to get us over the hump. "This is it!" they said. "We could update our system. It would only be about $75,000. Some of us don't like the system anyway, and if we got a new one, we could automate the process, and the issue would be solved."

This spurred a mental notification of a key takeaway from another meeting the week prior: We are contractually bound to our current system for the next three years, with no budget for alternatives. Again, with all the love in my heart, my response to the team was, "Unfortunately, that's not possible."

As I continued rejecting these "perfect" solutions my team was offering, I watched their energy evaporate. One frustrated team member finally confronted me and said, "Wait a second, this is a sick game. You ask us for ideas, we give you perfect solutions, and then your job is to shut down everything we suggest? Is that what leadership is? I'm not going to play this game anymore! I'm out. It's clear you don't value our input and opinions."

This painful cycle I went through repeats in organizations everywhere, created unwittingly when leaders invite teams to imagine solutions without framing the current reality the team is operating in.

Inviting team input is necessary in any business, but when the opinions are outside the bounds of reality, they become pie-in-the-sky suggestions with no possibility of being executed because they fly in the face of real business constraints. This is precisely why thinking *inside* the box proves so powerful, because it transforms the conversation entirely and ensures that everyone's input is channeled where it can be most impactful. It provides structure so people know where they can play.

But wouldn't it make more sense for leaders to focus on removing all the barriers?

A fascinating study involving schoolchildren and playgrounds answers this question and offers a profound lesson for leaders to get the most out of their team's creativity (see sidebar).

TELLING THE KIDS TO GO PLAY WHEREVER THEY WANT—A STUDY[6]

A group of children were taken to two distinct playgrounds, each supervised by a caregiver. The first playground was unbounded, while the second was enclosed by a see-through fence.

Conventional wisdom might suggest that the absence of boundaries would encourage the children to roam freely, their joy and creativity unleashed across the open area surrounding the park. Surprisingly, the opposite occurred. In the unfenced playground, the children remained clustered around their caregiver, hesitant and fearful to venture forth.

The fenced playground, however, yielded strikingly different behavior. Within the defined perimeter, the children began to explore extensively, using nearly every corner and piece of equipment. The presence of clear boundaries seemed to instill a sense of security, paradoxically fostering greater freedom, creativity, and adventurousness.

This observation holds valuable insights for organizations. Many assume that granting teams unrestricted freedom to think outside the box and removing barriers are the keys to unlocking innovation and creativity. However, much like the children in the study, teams often thrive when given well-defined parameters. In other words, people don't flourish in infinite possibility; they freeze.

Finding possibilities to move forward comes from clearly articulating the boundaries of the challenges at hand, not disregarding them. By establishing a "fence," be it budget constraints, timeline, specific objectives, or even the limiting beliefs being shared, leaders provide

---

6 Peter Summerlin, "Residential Design Award of Honor," American Society of Landscape Architects, ASLA 2006 Student Awards, 2006, https://www.asla.org/awards/2006/studentawards/282.html.

a framework within which creativity can thrive. This approach channels innovative thinking toward practical, implementable solutions.

In essence, the path to groundbreaking ideas often lies not in thinking outside the box but in thinking creatively within it. Innovation emerges when teams fully explore and push against the edges of their defined space, much like the children who found freedom within the fenced playground.

RBL's Thinking Inside the Box tool allows you to use this lesson to your advantage with your team. It clarifies and makes visual the known constraints and challenges. Thinking *inside* the boundaries of the situation is where true innovation and next right action lie. More important, thinking inside the box allows people to clearly see ideas that can be acted on within their area of influence without changing the external circumstances influencing them.

The tool is profound in its structure because it helps you hold the center in those conversations, without collusion, to open that space for breakthrough.

This reframing achieves something remarkable. It stops the endless argument with reality and redirects energy and input to what is genuinely possible *right now*. Any action that doesn't bump up against the established constraints and moves you even incrementally toward your goal becomes a valid next right action.

If your team is reciting a litany of barriers, excuses, or competing priorities for why they can't proceed, recognize it as your cue to begin drawing the box, and invite them to creatively think within it.

For anyone using the tool, this models in a real and practical way that circumstances aren't the reason you can't succeed but are the reality in which you *could*. The circumstances are our assignment, not our justification to not move forward. When you start to embrace and experience this truth, the path toward your goal continues to materialize.

HOW TO USE THE THINKING INSIDE THE BOX TOOL

Make sure you set up this tool on a large piece of paper, whiteboard, or virtual screen that the whole group can see. Write down all the responses, and avoid going through the exercise verbally.

1. **Define the Goal:** Start by clearly stating the outcome or goal you want to achieve. Keep it simple and specific, essentially, "What are we trying to accomplish?" Write the goal at the top of the page.
2. **Draw the Box:** Create a visual representation of the box.
3. **List the Constraints:** On either side of the box, start listing the constraints, barriers, excuses, circumstances, and reasons for why the person or team believes they can't take next right action. These can be real or perceived challenges or even limiting beliefs. There is no limit to the number of constraints on each side of the box, and there is no requirement as to what side to write them on. I typically alternate writing them on each side of the box as people share them. If the situation involves competing priorities or competing goals between departments, write each goal on either side of the box.
4. **Remind the Group:** State that for this tool, thinking outside the box leads to an argument with reality, and this exercise is about considering how we could move forward within our current circumstances. If you haven't yet, remember to validate the experience and feelings that this is in fact a challenging, difficult, or unforeseen situation the group is trying to navigate.
5. **Invite the In-the-Box Ideas:** Now that your goal is clear and your constraints are visible, ask, "Given our goal is XYZ and given these constraints or competing priorities, how could you move forward? Think inside the box."

Pro Tip: If the question causes silence or you feel the energy turned to you, I recommend changing your physical positioning to join the group and stare at the tool with them. This shifts the dynamic from you and the tool versus the audience and now positions you as on the same team and united against the problem outlined in the tool. If the conversation is one-to-one, try to sit down beside them and look at the tool on your piece of paper or screen.

1. **Capture Responses:** Write down every response shared. If new barriers or constraints come up, add them to the outside of the box to be considered. If an idea doesn't bump up against any constraints and theoretically could make progress toward the goal, add it inside the box as a possible next right action. If an idea is shared that you aren't sure fits as a constraint or next right action, make a list in a separate area that is your "need to find out more information" list, and let the group know you will seek those answers and return them to the tool as a constraint or idea once you find out.
2. **Get Commitments to Next Right Action:** Take the ideas in the box and ask, "Who would like to take action on this?" If the tool doesn't end with who, doing what, by when, it is as if it never happened. These commitments become an easy check-in to start your follow-up coaching conversation to monitor progress toward overcoming the unpreferred reality.

Digital Toolkit: Want to download this tool template and watch a tutorial video example? Scan the QR code. From the link, you can also download the full Call to Greatness Framework Toolkit.

Now with the tool outlined, let's look at a few examples where Thinking Inside the Box issued a call to greatness in one swoop. The following stories illustrate how to use the tool and why it's a secret weapon for you as a leader to unlock hidden innovation in your team.

Changing Everything Without Changing Anything

A nurse leader I'll call Molly approached me following a short training presentation I was doing at a large health-care system in Oregon. She had a problem. "I just can't get enough sleep," she said, with slumped shoulders and puffy eyes. "I swear no one in health care can get enough sleep right now because of the twelve- to fourteen-hour shifts we're required to work. With only twenty-four hours in the day, there's simply not enough time."

In Molly's view, the demands at work were unreasonable. Her belief that it was impossible to get enough sleep seemed unshakable. Her mindset often affected her mood as her shift began and sometimes leaked into her days off, when she could have been recharging.

As I read her energy in front of me, I had a sense there was an opportunity to invite some cleaner thinking around the sense she was making of this predicament. I also felt she might gain some insight regarding her part in the situation and her role in finding the solution, but in glancing at my watch, I realized I only had a few minutes before I was supposed to be speaking to another group at the hospital. Feeling that she had an open heart and willingness to try something new in her approach, I decided to take a risk and jump directly to an invitation to Thinking Inside the Box with her.

I started briefly with validating her experience and feelings: "It's completely understandable to feel drained. Balancing long shifts and constant demands isn't easy on anyone."

With her experience validated, I continued, "I'm not sure if I can easily solve this for you, but I may have a way to think through this challenge a bit differently that may help. Are you game?" She was. With the invitation accepted, the stage was set to see what next right actions might be hiding in plain sight.

I turned to the whiteboard in her break area and drew a box with the marker. At the top I wrote the goal. It looked something like this:

GOAL: GET MORE SLEEP		

"Yes, that is my goal," Molly said. I clarified: "You said the barriers that keep you from getting enough sleep are the twelve- to fourteen-hour shifts and that the day only has twenty-four hours?"

She nodded and continued to watch with curiosity. On one side of the box, I scribbled the constraint of "twelve- to fourteen-hour shifts." On the opposite side, I wrote the other constraint: "only twenty-four hours in a day." Now the box looked something like this:

GOAL: GET MORE SLEEP		
12- to 14-hour shifts		Only 24 hours in a day

We looked at the visual, and I asked, "Given that your goal is to get more sleep, and given that in a twenty-four-hour day, you work a twelve-hour shift, how could you get more sleep?"

As is common with the human condition, she began with outside-the-box thinking: "Well, they're having you do all this training and coaching. Maybe you could talk to the administration about changing these twelve-hour shifts. They're unreasonable and crazy. We're all suffering."

I said, "I could do that. Can you point out a senior leader in the administration who could change that policy? Whom should I talk to about this?"

She quickly shook her head and pulled me back as she realized that investing efforts in changing the entire shift structure in her organization was not the best use of our time and energy at this point. From there, I did some clarification and teaching: "I often see people focus on outside-the-box thinking, and that's an argument with reality that they lose. For now, let's play around with inside-the-box thinking, as I just drew. Your stated goal is more sleep, and given that you work twelve-hour shifts and there are only twenty-four hours in a day, how could *you* possibly start making progress toward your goal?"

Again, silence. Then I noticed she was getting annoyed, and the energy from this anger was projected at me. But I (the facilitator or leader) wasn't the issue, as I was momentarily there to help; it was her lack of sleep (clarified in the tool we had created). Noticing her emotional shift, I moved to stand beside her, shoulder to shoulder. This signified that we were on the same team working the problem together.

We stood together looking at the whiteboard, and I resisted the urge to break the silence. This shifted the energy to self-reflection about the issue we'd captured on the board, which was the real problem. After a few excruciating moments of additional silence, to my relief, a smile broke over her tired face.

Molly glanced at me and then shadowboxed a few punches at the tool on the wall. She said, "You know what? You're right. I could stop watching so much Netflix after work."

We both laughed as I wrote in the box, "Watch less Netflix." As Molly saw the solution didn't *need* to be found in changing external factors within the organization, the established schedules, or the amount of time in a day, she realized she'd always had the power to achieve her goal. She said, "I am now realizing how often I just zone out in my car after my shift, doomscrolling on social media and losing track of time. I could just make a habit of putting down my phone after my shift and heading home to sleep."

I wrote, "Put phone down after shift." Now the box looked like this:

GOAL: GET MORE SLEEP		
12–14 hour shifts	√ Watch less Netflix √ Put phone down after work	Only 24 hour days in a day

As we wrapped up, I asked Molly to choose one idea she was willing to commit to (the first step of accountability), and she pointed to "Put phone down after work." I scribbled a "yes" next to that idea to signify her commitment to action. We shared one last laugh as I left to start the next training session.

In less than ten minutes, she'd come up with realistic solutions to her dilemma that were within the bounds of her reality and would achieve her goal of more sleep. If we'd had more time, we probably could have come up with a dozen inside-the-box ideas.

In this situation, Molly realized that her job, her bosses, and the organization weren't keeping her from her sleep goal. She had been using her circumstances as an excuse to keep from taking the necessary actions to achieve her goal.

This lesson becomes an interesting pattern the more you complete thinking-inside-the-box reflections and act. The reasons and excuses fueling "why you can't" simply become the constraints to consider in pursuit of your goal. In my experience, without exception, an opportunity to move toward "how you could" appears inside the box.

Going for an Impossible Goal

At Reality-Based Leadership, we routinely use this tool, especially when we have a goal that seems undoable. For example, one day our founder returned from a business trip and made a startling announcement: "I want my own TV show."

The team was taken aback and sheepishly asked, "You mean like Oprah, but for business and leadership development?" She said, "Yes! Exactly that."

Surprised as we were by the audacious goal set, she then proceeded to level up the challenge by sharing the constraints we'd have to consider in achieving the goal: The show would have to be budget neutral. Because her schedule was overstuffed with business development meetings, speaking engagements, and coaching clients, she wanted minimal involvement in the planning. Her travel schedule was hectic, so no engaging a production company or traveling to a studio. We couldn't hire additional staff, even though none of us had the skills or experience for producing a TV show. She didn't want scripts either; she wanted to stick to her spontaneous speaking style.

Our team, normally quick to sprint with an idea, looked at her in stunned silence. She was putting up limits to every resource needed to create a successful TV show.

For weeks, team members scheduled time to scan the internet and look for resources we hadn't thought of, hoping to discover innovative ways to meet her goal. After a few weeks, our conversations veered over into the "why we can't" lane supported by a hefty amount of complaining. It became clear it was time to run the idea through The Call to Greatness Framework if we were to find any relief or clear ways forward.

In working our way through the steps of the framework as a team, we gained clarity on the situation, accountability for our lack of solutions thus far, and defined our role in making it happen. However, next right action to possibly creating this TV show still wasn't clear. With the team stuck, what tool would be best for discovering possible next right actions?

With a clear goal already set and initial constraints shared explicitly with the team, it was a no-brainer that the Thinking Inside the Box tool would be the perfect starting point.

We visually set up the Thinking Inside the Box tool anchored in our current reality.

GOAL: COMPANY TV SHOW		
Budget neutral No more of CEO's time Minimal planning No $$ for production company or studio Use current staff No studio acoustics or formal set	Given this, how could we?	Current staff lacks TV show skill sets No scripts Currently lack equipment: video cameras, microphones, professional lighting, etc.

As often happens, frustration with the constraints led to initial arguments with reality as our team veered into thinking outside the box. Someone said, "Surely we should be able to hire at least *one person* who actually knows how to produce a show." Our facilitator pointed to the constraint: *No extra staff.* Someone else argued, "Come on! She must take time out of the day to do this. Let's ask if she can just put some time in her schedule."

A colleague saw that suggestion bump up against another constraint: "Look, the reality is that she doesn't want the show to take more time in her day."

Without a breakthrough, team members snapped a picture and sent out the visual as an assignment to reflect on over the next few days. We'd return to the exercise later in the week.

Soon after, I was home watching a Facebook video on my phone after a long workday. I glanced at my wife, who also was watching a video on her phone. Then I looked at the TV hanging on the wall. It was off. In fact, it was usually off.

I moved next to my wife to see what she was watching: a makeup tutorial on YouTube, which had been out for two days and already had eight million views. I had been watching an entrepreneur giving advice, which boasted two million views. A quick internet search of "How many views did Oprah get on her show at its peak?" yielded a result showing between ten million and twelve million viewers.

An idea sparked that could fit our inside-the-box scenario. We had been "watching TV" on our phones. Couldn't we create a "TV show" like the ones we'd just been watching?

At our next meeting, I shared my idea with the team. We could create videos in our own Reality-Based Leadership style! Who needed a production company? The organization provided us with camera phones, and we all were capable of shooting video. YouTube had plenty of tutorials on how to get the best shots and edit video. As for content, people were constantly approaching the company founder after she presented keynote speeches, and she always had a team member with her to provide help and support at events. That person could capture the content as she went about her day and bring it back for editing.

Once we stopped arguing with reality and stayed inside the box, innovation emerged. The tool had dissolved the resistance to the constraints and lack of resources we'd believed would keep us from meeting the goal. It took a while, but we moved from "why we can't" to "how we could." The visual box diagram we'd begun was soon flooded with input and ideas from team members in support of our founder's goal. This not only skyrocketed our energy; it also ensured alignment to the goal and an eventual next right action to execute as we assigned out commitments for each in-the-box idea.

In less than two weeks, our team had created the show *Life's Messy, Live Happy* for our founder. The show eventually got one hundred thousand views and listens per month across all our platforms and became a fan favorite. The result simultaneously fulfilled the goal of our CEO and taught our team a valuable lesson: that even the most impossible-sounding goals are achievable if the Thinking Inside the Box tool is involved.

Competing Priorities and Goals Between Departments

A market research technology company, trying to scale its business, butted up against a common organizational sinkhole: conflict between the sales and marketing teams. This fight over priorities had gone on for years. The groups were so locked into their departmental goals that the fact they were all on the same team got lost. Drama had boiled over and was stunting the growth of the organization and the ability to find a way forward.

Senior leaders had directed the marketing department to be laser focused about ensuring that marketing collateral, proposals, quotes, and so on were on brand. Everything that went out—emails, presentations, promotional collateral—had to pass through the marketing department's standards process to ensure that materials had the correct logo, colors, and design. The company's branding standards were nonnegotiable, and providing on-demand materials would put a stress on staff time and risk an off-brand message going out.

The sales department saw the marketing department's mission as obstructing its goals. Sales reps said they sometimes needed quick access to updated visuals, pamphlets, and other materials that could influence customers—especially if they had a ready-to-buy prospect. Because of the marketing approval process, the sales team worried it wouldn't immediately have the materials and support needed to take advantage of hot sales leads. They feared they would lose business and miss ambitious revenue goals.

Both departments had worthy goals and concerns. Everyone wanted to be successful in their efforts. However, conflict and finger-pointing arose when the goals seemingly clashed. They viewed each other as enemies and obstacles and often cited each other as an excuse for "why we can't" achieve goals.

We frequently see this adversarial attitude among departments when we work with organizations: sales versus operations, leaders versus staff, faculty versus administration, nursing versus administration, and—my favorite joke—IT versus everyone.

Thinking Inside the Box is a means to turn the challenge away from arguing about whose needs or goals are more important ("why we can't") and refocuses everyone on the shared goal of the business ("how we could"). The process elevates thinking and reminds departments that they are allies, not enemies.

Here is how it resolved the conflict between the marketing and sales departments at this technology organization.

After drawing the box, we wrote the marketing goal and focus on the left side of the box: "Everything on brand." The sales team goal was "marketing materials on a timely basis when needed." We then asked, "What is the overarching goal that you're *both* going for that fits into the larger organization's goals?" We were essentially asking, *What are both departments trying to do here?*

After reflection and discussion, both sides agreed to the overarching goal—increasing sales and growing the business—which turned the groups toward each other, reminding them they were on the same team! The box looked like this:

GOAL: INCREASE SALES/GROW THE BUSINESS		
Marketing: Everything on brand and through process		Sales: Timely access to new marketing materials and collateral

The teams had a visual representation of their common goal and could see how each hoped to contribute. Marketing used its expertise toward growth by focusing on branding, and sales felt a legitimate need for quick access to marketing materials to secure sales. The fear of sales hijacking the branding process was on the table for marketing, and the fear of not having the necessary promotional materials to sell was clear for the sales group.

"Given that marketing's goal is to have everything on brand, and sales' goal is to have timely and easy access to materials periodically, how could our shared goal of growing the business be achieved?" I asked.

As often happens, people launched into an outside-the-box argument with reality. Sales: "Marketing shouldn't be so rigid about their fancy branding processes and just give us what we need when we need it." Marketing: "Sales can just sell what they have and quit making excuses that they need customized material all the time."

I reminded them to suggest ideas that fell within the constraints set by the two departments. That began an awkward silence. I moved to standing among the two groups so we could look at the tool together. In this positioning, we were all now united looking at the problem together.

Finally, someone from the marketing department suggested, "We could create a kind of 'bank account' that sales could use to bypass our process and get something quickly. Like maybe five 'asks' per quarter for us to make something specialized they need urgently, and that would be bumped to priority. We could do something fun to keep track, like giving each salesperson five Monopoly dollars. Once they are out of their fake dollars, they must use what they already have or follow standard process. That would create a boundary for us in marketing and alleviate sales' fear of not having what they need when they need it."

After fleshing out the idea, the group was not only committed to the plan; they were also excited. Salespeople were happy to use Monopoly dollars to get what they wanted, and they could acknowledge the stress these requests put on the marketing team. This innovative collaboration acknowledged competing goals while protecting the overall organizational goal.

For years, leadership had tried and failed to alleviate the tension between the departments. By thinking inside the box, the two departments came up with their own creative solution that everyone was committed to following.

Over the next two quarters, something interesting happened. The Monopoly dollars were mostly unspent. The real breakthrough came as one staffer spent all five of his dollars in two weeks! This illuminated something about the crux of the conflict.

The individual who used his dollars quickly discovered a personal development opportunity. He was disorganized and had refused to get fluent in technology and internal systems, which caused him to reach out for all of these one-off pieces of collateral from marketing. Although he'd been a top salesperson, he was unfamiliar with the internal system technology, where most of what he wanted had already been created and was available. Instead of prolonging the ongoing battle between sales and marketing, the Thinking Inside the Box tool gave leaders the needed reference point and clarity to finally call out and coach the individual who had been resisting the use of the internal system to become more fluent.

Managing Energy in a Crisis and Critical Moments

It was the height of the COVID-19 pandemic in 2020, and the times were still calling for masking, wiping down groceries, and social distancing wherever you went. A governmental agency that was heavily involved in the response to this global crisis was on the conference line in our office, desperately seeking help with a challenge that seemed impossible.

Admittedly scared, discombobulated, and, like everyone else, trying to process the chaos of what was transpiring across the world, I huddled at the conference table alongside my fellow speaker at RBL, trying to orient to the situation. Our longtime client from Washington, DC, for whom we'd conducted leadership development programs, was facing a predicament caused by a recent mandate from their decision-makers.

Flipping the conversation to speakerphone, the leaders began sharing the chilling details of what they had been tasked with. Fearful and struggling with all the uncertainty of the continuously evolving situation, they had reached out to RBL for advice on how to proceed.

This leadership group had been told they'd be required to return to the office a few days each pay period, even as the pandemic was raging on. Amid all the uncertainty, this mandate would require three hundred people to show up on the seventh floor of their building by 8:00 a.m. The decision was nonnegotiable and critical for the American citizens they supported, and they had two weeks to prepare.

The group was seething in frustration and fear—and rightly so, given the circumstances. We were hearing an onslaught of arguments about why this request was unreasonable—even impossible. People were saying things like, "I swear they don't care about our health and well-being. This is completely unacceptable and dangerous. They don't value our safety at all!"

Others continued by sharing the glaring and, to them, obvious reasons why this order wouldn't be possible to carry out: "There is still so much uncertainty about the virus. Information is changing daily. We can only have four people on the elevator at a time because of social distancing requirements. There aren't enough elevators for that number of people. The stairs are currently not an option, so there will be egregious wait times at the elevator. We don't currently have masks for three hundred people. The requirement is to wipe down buttons and sanitize high-touch areas, and there is a back order on hand sanitizer. There are worries about inadequate health and safety measures in the cafeteria. People want guarantees their employer had thought of everything so they would be safe from infection. Some of the public transit in DC is under travel restrictions. The desks! The way they are designed and structured, there will be too much exposure to each other. What if someone gets sick and comes into work, giving it to others?"

The more team members shared, the more dire the situation felt.

Listening in, my shoulders felt high enough to touch my ears, and a lump was gathering in my throat.

As my attention returned to the phone in the center of the table, my gaze shifted to a sketch that my colleague was creating as the group continued talking. It seemed to me like an odd time to be doodling, but then I realized she had been writing word-for-word the challenges the team was sharing that would make it impossible to fulfill the request. It was the beginning sketch of a Thinking Inside the Box tool to anchor the group! With each new circumstance introduced, she'd write it down with a grimace, almost as if nursing a pulled muscle.

At the top of the paper, the sketch read, "GOAL: Within two weeks, three hundred people, safely on the seventh floor at 8:00 a.m." Underneath that, a box. On the right and left side of the almost-finished box were the twenty-plus issues that the group had brought up. A recreation of that sketch follows.

GOAL: 300 PEOPLE, SAFELY ON THE SEVENTH FLOOR AT 8:00 A.M. IN TWO WEEKS		
CONSTRAINTS?		**CONSTRAINTS?**
Uncertainty about the virus		Don't currently have enough masks
Could possibly get sick		Only four at a time in the elevator
Shortage of hand sanitizer		Unable to use stairs due to distancing requirements
Challenges in atrium design for large number of people to gather at same time		Six feet distancing required
Some public transit has limitations		Some staff has ambulatory challenges
Office space isn't designed for distancing		Virus could be spread at desk without barriers
Buttons on elevator must be sanitized each trip		Currently, decision is made a mandate
Concerns about health and safety measures in cafeteria		Can't guarantee all safety measures can be taken all the time; information changes daily
May be egregious wait times at elevators		Not enough elevators for three hundred people

After nearly fifteen minutes of back-and-forth, silence finally took the stand.

On our end, it felt as if a fog of "why we can't" and "why we shouldn't have to" had pushed the oxygen out of our office. It reminded me of playing high-school baseball growing up in the humid Iowa summers, when the air was so thick you almost had to chew through it.

After letting that silence breathe, I'll never forget what happened next.

My colleague began, "Team, I want to start with validating this experience you all are having. I can see that all of us are scared, many of us are upset, and some are downright ticked. This is a highly unpreferred reality you've found yourself in. We can all agree this is simply not ideal.

"I would like to throw something out there, and it doesn't mean we have to act yet. Given this unpreferred reality, and given our goal is to have all three hundred people on the team on the seventh floor by 8:00 a.m. in two weeks, and given our constraints . . ." Then she proceeded to read word for word every challenge she had written on the sketch from her paper and finished with, "How could we make this happen? What if we could?"

There was a stunned disbelief that the question was being asked. A tense silence filled the room.

It continued.

And continued some more.

Finally, after what seemed like an hour, a voice from the other end of the line trickled through: "I do know a family friend, a dentist, who may have unused masks, and we could get those until the shortage is alleviated. There may be similar professions we could reach out to as well."

We frantically scribbled the first idea inside the box on the sketch.

Another individual jumped in: "I suppose we could create a simple scheduling spreadsheet that is tiered so people aren't all showing up right at 7:50 a.m. and crowding into the atrium of the building, thus increasing the chance of exposure to the virus."

Before she finished, another exclaimed, "I'd be happy to leave a half hour early on my commute to support this idea!"

In jumped another: "I had accidentally ordered five large hand sanitizers from Amazon about a month ago instead of two. I'd be happy to bring in my three extras to help create hand hygiene stations at the first floor and seventh floor."

The momentum continued: "My husband has a friend who works in fiberglass manufacturing, and they could come and set up temporary barriers around desk areas."

In a powerful moment, one individual confessed, "I realize I have been asking for a guarantee that I won't get sick from the virus. I can commit to wearing my mask, good hand hygiene, and distancing while on-site. I can follow the evidence of what can keep me safe and live with the calculated risks that everyone else is accepting as well."

The ideas continued, one after another, inspired by the self-reflection baked into the tool and the way it united everyone to focus together on the problem. The fixation on "why we can't" had evaporated, and energy was being channeled into "how we could" given the unprecedented challenge they were facing. The tool was able to lovingly and courageously hold the center as people's minds and egos initially went to fearful extremes.

If the suggestions didn't bump up against the constraints of the unpreferred realities listed on the outside of the box, they were added inside the box as ideas for next right action.

This courageous, resourceful group realized a powerful core truth of Reality-Based Leadership that forever stuck with them: Even your unprecedented circumstances aren't the reason you can't succeed but the reality in which you must succeed.

The experience ended with commitments from team members to act on the inside-the-box suggestions.

The result? Two weeks later, the team succeeded in their goal of everyone operating safely from the seventh floor. By embracing the profound shift in group thinking, they succeeded despite challenging circumstances. This group had moved from "why we can't" to "how we could." Most important, this experience showed that even during the immense pressure associated with leading during a crisis and unprecedented times, the RBL tools can open a path toward next right action.

Using the Tool When Faced with the "Sucker's Choice"

Leaders often are confronted with questions such as these:

"Do you want it done quickly **OR** with high quality?"

"Do you want us to find new clients **OR** serve current customers?"

"Do you want a reliable process **OR** creative flexibility?"

"Do you want us to coach people **OR** make sure they get the work done?"

"Do you want productivity **OR** work–life balance?"

At RBL, we call this the "sucker's choice," and Thinking Inside the Box helps people move away from such either-or thinking. The underlying assumption of the sucker's choice is that one goal can't be achieved without sacrificing the other. Of course, trade-offs and balance are natural, but either-or thinking blinds us to the many possibilities that exist along the spectrum between the two extremes. Thinking Inside the Box renders those possibilities for next right action visible by finding the *and* in the situation.

When you hear people falling for the sucker's choice, draw the box. Refer to the organization's major goals or company values at the top: Increase revenue, focus on customer satisfaction, delight customers, maintain (employee) safety, and so on. Then outline the two either-or options that are being presented as mutually exclusive. Ideas that land inside the box, if they are within the boundaries or constraints, are often worthy solutions or intentional next steps.

Here's how you may start this conversation: "I notice you're seeing this as an either-or situation. I'd like to invite you to consider what would happen if we swapped out the *or* for *and*. Given that an organizational goal is to always delight the customer, and given we'd like to do that by creating products that are extremely high-quality, and given that we'd love to deliver it to our customers quickly, how could we make that happen?"

GOAL: DELIGHT OUR CUSTOMERS		
High-quality?	How could we? Find the sweet spot.	Done quickly?

Then let the silence do its work. I've facilitated this exercise hundreds of times, and an individual or team almost always comes up with at least one action step. Many are obvious answers. I've heard, "You mean I should more consistently follow the project management methodology I've *already* been trained in?" Or, "I should build better relationships with external partners involved in the execution?" And, "I should learn how to delegate and stop believing I'm the only one who can do this?" In other words, the tool often reveals a call to greatness to improve a skill set, modernize an approach, or increase willingness to act using the support tools and resources already at your disposal.

The answer to moving both worthy goals forward springs from addressing the tension held with the Thinking Inside the Box tool.

What to Watch Out for When Thinking Inside the Box

Thinking Inside the Box provides a springboard for helping people, teams, or departments get unstuck. The more you think inside the box, the more you and your team will realize that the circumstances outside of the box need far less changing. The tool acknowledges an unpreferred reality, allows leaders to validate the experience, and ends the argument between reality and "why we can't" excuses. Most of all, energy shifts quickly into "how we could" take next right action. Here are tips for getting the maximum benefit from the tool.

- Again, the tool works best when done in writing, either on paper or a whiteboard. It can also be done virtually with a spreadsheet,

PowerPoint slide, or template. Using this tool verbally is likely to ignite the ego.

- Facilitators and leaders should resist the urge to offer their inside-the-box ideas or solutions before the individual or group does. Offering ideas could make it appear you are leading the group to your preferences and ideas. If you use the exercise as a tool for manipulation, it won't work. If the group is stuck for ideas and you would like to offer one of your own, do it as an invitation like this: "I have an idea that could possibly work; would you like to hear it?" If the group says they do, offer your idea, and then step back for the team to continue the remaining ideas.
- When people talk about "why they can't" or add additional issues or excuses, it's imperative to list that as a constraint on the visual tool. Whatever is said out loud by those participating either goes inside the box as an idea for next right action or outside the box as an additional constraint. Not writing down an idea can be viewed as the leader not listening or disregarding an idea or concern. If it is unclear whether the idea is a constraint, create a separate list and let the team know that you will investigate whether that is an organizational constraint.
- The Thinking Inside the Box tool is easy to set up, but it can take time and energy to agree on the true goal and constraints. Using high-level organizational goals that are common in every industry (e.g., growth, safety, customer satisfaction, user experience, and efficiency) can be a good way to anchor people on a shared goal. It reminds everyone they're on the same team and should be operating in the spirit of what's best for the organization, not personal preferences.

- If you use the Thinking Inside the Box tool with departments with competing goals, both groups should clarify and agree on company goals (listed at the top of the tool) and individual goals (listed on the sides of the tool).
- If the facilitator or leader thinks a constraint is unwarranted based on their knowledge or perspective (e.g., being "short-staffed" when the data show staffing levels are adequate), add it to the list anyway. If the group believes it's an obstacle, it is. The tool's design will still support the mindset shift by wrapping in the constraint and focusing everyone on possible helpful actions: "Given that believed barrier, how could you . . . ?"
- If a constraint on the tool is later found to no longer be a constraint—for example, new resources are found—cross it out.
- Learn to be comfortable with silence. If you're in front of the room, go stand among the group to look at the Thinking Inside the Box tool with them, which will subtly signal that you are part of the team, not the person preventing them from getting what they need.
- Silence also can signal it's time for a break and moves the tool into an assignment for self-reflection. A script I like to use is this: "Thank you for your participation and for our progress so far. Let's keep thinking on this one. I'll take a picture and email this to everyone, and we'll meet at the end of the week for more inside-the-box ideas."
- Silence also can reveal a lack of willingness to do what it takes given the current reality the team is facing. Leaders can only work with the willing. If the situation is appropriate, you can say, "Now that we know addressing the problem is doable but we just lack willingness, we can rest a little easier knowing that

at least we've identified the true issue." I recommend making a copy of the tool you've completed so far and sending it out to the team to work with until the next gathering. Encourage them to reflect on the tool, ask others for their inside-the-box ideas, or even reach out to their network of contacts to see whether they have any ideas. This crowdsourcing of ideas with the visual tool as an anchor can break through that lack of willingness as others insert their ideas that fit in the box. It can also be effective to feed the completed structure of Thinking Inside the Box into an AI tool (such as ChatGPT) and ask it to provide ideas that would suffice inside the box without bumping up against the constraints. After all, there is one thing that AI doesn't lack—the willingness to offer additional ideas for "how we could."

- If people change the subject or identify other difficult issues related to the problem, create a separate Thinking Inside the Box as a parking lot. Then turn the focus back to the initial issue. This shows that people are being listened to, and the challenges can be addressed later without losing momentum on the original goal.
- Sharing a written inside-the-box graphic with decision-makers can be a great strategy for demonstrating accountability and willingness to acknowledge constraints. Decision-makers might identify additional constraints. Once they are all clearly visible, a single inside-the-box idea can be the breakthrough. Additionally, decision-makers who see the efforts of your team trying to innovate given the constraints are often more prone to remove a key barrier that your team identifies through the exercise.
- If you are leading teams remotely, use the whiteboard features, try a second camera integration on your computer, or access

RBL's digital toolkit templates to build these tools in front of your team. Follow this QR code to download those templates.

- A final lesson is that the better you get at thinking inside the box and succeeding despite circumstances, the better equipped you are to see what needs to be shifted outside the box. Those that consistently find breakthroughs and move toward goals from inside-the-box thinking become credible witnesses in their organization when they ask for a specific exception or to remove a barrier that's holding them back.

The Thinking Inside the Box tool is also the best tool selection if you are sensing that your team or someone is

- Pointing to circumstances as reasons why they can't proceed
- Facing constraints or known barriers to moving toward a goal
- Lacking immediate resources (e.g., time, money, tools, staff, or support)
- Making excuses for "why they can't"
- Waiting for perfect conditions to begin
- Facing limitations (perceived or known)
- Caught in limiting beliefs
- Navigating competing priorities or competing goals

Remember: Thinking Inside the Box is a great tool for getting unstuck and revealing next right action. It reduces conflict and creates a venue for productive compromise and collaboration. The tool reveals that circumstances are the reality in which you can succeed. It simultaneously validates people's experience and extends an invitation to reconsider the sense they are making of it. It is the perfect balance of loving your people up and calling them up to greatness.

It is also a pain reliever, because it shifts perspectives from a messy or impossible challenge to productive actions that can be taken within established business boundaries.

I've heard time and again that this tool restores hope and gives courage to leaders to address tough leadership challenges. A Thinking Inside the Box habit helps people see that a way forward is always available. It gets them out of the either-or thinking that limits possibilities.

While it doesn't promise a guaranteed fast track to the final solution, it simultaneously invites engagement, fuels personal accountability, and unlocks innovation hidden in plain sight.

CHAPTER 7

NEGATIVE BRAINSTORMING

If the SBAR is best for those who aren't sure where to start and Thinking Inside the Box is for those who can't find a way forward because of constraints, the Negative Brainstorming tool is your go-to when you notice your team is overwhelmed, overthinking, or paralyzed by fear because of a business change.

Once fear takes hold of someone's thinking, they get overly focused on the daunting list of tasks required to achieve their goal and fixate on the barriers in their way. They feel like they can't plan for everything so why try anything, and this reinforces a state of being stuck. This solidifies the belief that the path ahead is insurmountable given the issues in the way. The result is a doubling down on "why they can't" in the short term and, if left unaddressed, a mindset of resistance to change in the future.

It becomes a vicious cycle.

The truth is that most people do not want to resist change at work or wish to hinder their ability to innovate when faced with an unpreferred reality. However, this is what often happens when people are not provided a space to channel that fearful energy and concern into intentional next steps.

While there are always valid concerns and input that need consideration for how to intentionally move forward, many of these concerns should not become excuses for inaction.

Often, the unpreferred reality the team is standing toe-to-toe with must be dealt with, whether they like it or not. The decision is made, the issue that needs attention is in front of us, or the strategy is set.

In these situations, in which resistance is building with a cascade of concerns from those you lead, the Negative Brainstorming tool is where to turn for support. It creates a structured space where fears can be captured, acknowledged, examined, discussed with civility among the team, and ultimately transformed into more neutral strategic considerations. By providing a safe place to land for what might otherwise remain as unspoken worries, this tool allows valid concerns to be shared openly, fostering discussion and healthy dialogue while maintaining a focus on how to move forward.

Negative Brainstorming helps leaders address resistance and, counterintuitively, put fearful energy to good use by rechanneling it into next right action. The tool reveals that change at work doesn't have to be hard; it just tends to be hard for the unready.

By using the tool to deliberately explore what could go wrong, teams actually build confidence and clarity in their ability to proceed in spite of what may look messy and uncertain ahead. When fears are named and addressed directly, any remaining fog causing inaction lifts. This tool takes employees' legitimate concerns or fears into consideration, then simply reframes them as risks that could possibly deter or derail the team from achieving business goals. It shows that these potential roadblocks are not the reason we can't proceed but the reality in which we must.

HOW TO USE THE NEGATIVE BRAINSTORMING TOOL

Get started by grabbing a flip chart, whiteboard, spreadsheet, or even a sheet of paper—something visible for the group to see and contribute to. If done virtually, an Excel spreadsheet works also.

1. **Clarify the Change, Decision, or Unpreferred Reality:** At the top, clearly write out the change request, decision, or unpreferred reality as a heading for all to see. An example might be, "Everyone following the new documentation process with 100 percent compliance by February." This begins to set the stage for the group to reflect and focus on "how we could" and acknowledge, for the time being, that the decision has already been made and the organization isn't going back on it.
2. **Capture the Issues:** Just below the change, decision, or unpreferred reality you've clarified, write "ISSUES" in bold letters. Ask the group to get "good and negative" by naming everything they believe is standing in the way of success or that could go wrong with the change. Validate their experience with a simple statement like this: "There's a lot to consider with this <decision, change>, and I can see there's frustration or uncertainty. Let's list every issue that makes this hard to say yes to what is keeping us from our next right action." Prompt specific examples (e.g., instead of "not enough resources," say, "two people on paid time off for two weeks"). Write issues word for word without editing or solving them. Once the list is complete (and it will likely be long and heavy), thank them, and move to Step 3.

continued

3. **Reframe the Discussion:** Cross out "ISSUES," and label the list "RISKS." While doing so, it helps to tell the group, "Thank you for sharing the risks with this <decision, change>." Add two columns next to each risk: "PROBABILITY" (will this actually happen?) and "IMPACT" (if it does happen, what's the effect on the business, customers, clients, or patients?). Tell the group, "Before we discuss solutions, let's assess each risk based on how probable it is to happen and how much it would impact the business or those we serve if it did." This step reframes the discussion of emotion and personal preferences as organizational impact and potential.
4. **Evaluate and Discuss:** For each risk, invite the group to rate probability and impact as *high*, *medium*, or *low*. Encourage people to verbally throw out their vote. If opinions vary, note the difference; allow people to share their perspectives and reasons why. If there is ongoing disagreement, I suggest keeping the peace as a facilitator and mark it *medium*. The goal isn't precision; it's to surface collective insight. Encourage open discussion: "I heard a *low* and a *high* vote. Can each elaborate on their thinking?" Be sure to arrive at the probability and impact of *every* risk before moving on to the next step.
5. **Prioritize Which Risks to Focus On:** As the group assigns risk probability and impact, the Negative Brainstorming tool will start to look like this:

RISKS	PROBABILITY	IMPACT (ON THE BUSINESS)
Example one	high	medium
Example two	medium	high
Example three	low	low
Example four	high	high
Example five	low	low
Example six	high	high

6. Once the ratings are in, cross out the items rated *low* in both probability and impact. Visually, this reduces the clutter and brings relief because it symbolizes that the group has taken care of some concerns simply by taking the time to work through the tool. Then, circle the risks rated *high* under both columns—these are the priorities that warrant attention.
7. **Consider the True Risks of Next Right Action:** Start with the first *high–high* risk. Ask, "What are three things we could do to reduce or prepare for this risk?" Keep in mind that it isn't only about risk mitigation. Other ideas are to accept the risk, eliminate the risk, transfer the risk, insure against the risk, build contingencies, or monitor the risk. Depending on the group's mindset, expect idea sharing and creative problem-solving or silence; both are productive. In teams in which the latter is dominant, allow for silence and self-reflection, even if the time extends uncomfortably. In worst-case scenarios, the silence reveals where a team may be needing to update their skill set, modernize their approach, or revisit their level of willingness to do what their organization needs. After listing two to three actions per risk, assign ownership: "Who will take this one on?" Write down the person or group next to the action, along with a timeline of when they expect to complete it. This is where real accountability and buy-in starts.

Final Note: If the group feels it is necessary to complete any other risks that may be rated *medium* and *high*, go ahead and do so.

In every organization, this tool surfaces real concerns, filters the noise of "why we can't," and generates focused action. And it works every time.

continued

Digital Toolkit: Want to download this tool template and watch a tutorial video of it in action? Scan the QR code. You can also get the full Call to Greatness Framework at the link provided.

Participants, especially if immersed in drama, tend to focus on how risks affect their preferences or comfort zones. However, personal preferences cannot trump business potential. The tool gently and respectfully illuminates this key truth.

Negative Brainstorming dissipates much of the ambiguity and anxiety that accompanies change by clarifying the business risks, discussing them in detail, and assigning commitments for next right actions.

THE FULL CALL TO GREATNESS IN ACTION—VIRAL ON TIKTOK

When it came to reevaluating RBL's social media strategy, the SBAR tool provided a way to reveal high-level pathways for our founder to make a decision. Once the path was chosen, however, the situation called for a second next right action tool for clarity and intentional decision-making about where the team would best put their energy.

Concerns immediately arose within the team about how this decision would affect our clients and their experience of our content online, as well as the foundational paths on which new fans would get connected with our leadership tips. There was even fear within the team about how we would manage this decision while still supporting many of our current clients and fans who were accustomed to finding our work on their preferred platform over the years.

With the team beginning to blurt out several "if we do X, then X will trigger this issue and that issue," you could feel the tension and overwhelm rising. This familiar feeling within a group calls for the Negative Brainstorming tool as a way to support these concerns while eventually opening a window in the discussion to "how we could" given these concerns.

Our team threw a flip chart paper on the wall and began documenting every issue that had been shared, along with the additional challenges brought up as the brainstorm continued. The Negative Brainstorm about the change that had just been decided by our founder was in full effect.

By the end of the initial phase of the dialogue, all concerns had been moved from the team's heads onto paper.

The tides had turned from ambiguity to initial clarity. The unpreferred reality was now in front of us for the entire team to see. We were all united and looking at the same version of the problem. From there, we discussed each issue and narrowed down the probability that each concern would *actually* happen and the impact on our clients or fans if it did happen.

This anchor allowed for healthy disagreement and fact sharing about the *actual* probability and impact on our clients with each risk.

Here is a modified version of what the Negative Brainstorm looked like at this point, with PROBABILITY and IMPACT labels of low (L), medium (M), and high (H):

continued

ISSUE/CONCERN	PROBABILITY	IMPACT
Current email campaigns for clients link to social media posts that may be taken down	M	M
Current followers rely on social media for new content and tips from us and won't have that access	H	H
Some links could be broken on these campaigns after taking them down	L	M
Fans may think our founder retired	L	H
Fans may think she passed away	L	H
~~Calls may increase to office looking for content~~	~~L~~	~~L~~
~~Questions may increase about why we aren't posting~~	~~M~~	~~L~~
Marketing materials at speaking engagements tell new fans to follow us on platforms where we will be posting less	H	M
Current marketing collateral doesn't say to follow us on newsletter or podcast—where we want people to go now	H	H
Current website copy doesn't say to follow us on newsletter and podcast	M	M
~~Landing pages for people to sign up for our latest content direct people to social channels, not podcast and newsletter specifically~~	~~L~~	~~L~~
Website customer experience isn't directed to marketing channels we want now	H	L
PowerPoint slides for speaking events now direct audience to incorrect platforms	H	H
Newsletter currently gets half the meeting time of the team in comparison with social strategy	H	H

The team first crossed out anything that had been deemed low probability and low impact, and this immediately felt relieving and productive. It honestly felt as if we had knocked a few steps of work out by not doing anything at all, because the initial phases of the Negative Brainstorming process filtered out some reactive thinking about concerns that wouldn't make much difference in the grand scheme of things.

Then, the focus turned to tackling each one of the high-probability and high-impact risks given this decision and creating our plan for action. The question embedded in the tool was then proposed to our group: "Given this risk, what three things can we do to mitigate it or move forward?"

After a brief reflection, the ideas began flowing.

These were our next right action ideas for the risk that our current followers relied on social media for new content and tips from us and wouldn't have that access:

1. Our founder will create a series of informal educational videos about where to find our latest and most up-to-date content (now LinkedIn, our podcast, and newsletter).
2. Announce this shift to other platforms in our next newsletter in a creative way.
3. Change the QR codes at upcoming keynotes that direct people to follow us on social platforms and update that message based on the new strategy.

This last idea above connected to several others regarding our marketing at speaking engagements. The next risk was PowerPoint slides for speaking engagements now directing our new interest from the audience to incorrect platforms. These next steps involved creating a new slide

continued

and QR code with the link and modifying the landing page when the code was scanned.

On completion, the tool called out the risk that our team spent a great deal of time on social media content creation and strategy and a smaller percentage of time on preparing and strategizing our newsletter content. The risk identified was that the newsletter currently gets half the meeting time of the team in comparison with social strategy.

The ideas that the group came up with to mitigate this risk were as follows:

1. Do an audit of what newsletters performed well based on title, structure, content, etc.
2. Set structured time on the calendar for key people involved in building the newsletter.
3. Research favorite newsletters to brainstorm innovative ideas to elevate the newsletter experience for our fans.

The team finished the ideation phase for the rest of the tool and then moved into commitments. The final question posed by the team was, "Who would like to commit and take action on these ideas?"

Commitments were divvied up across our small team, each ending with who, doing what, and by when. These became easy follow-up check-in references, and the visual work of the tool remained in our shared working area. The team referred to it often to update progress over the next few months.

In the end, our team was able to conserve the energy that would have been lost arguing with the unpreferred reality and fighting the decision and instead channeled it into next right action and execution given the real concerns ahead.

The strategy was successfully shifted and implemented with speed, intention, and precision. Our fans easily found us on our new prioritized platforms, and, best of all, we were able to manage the branding risk that our previous approach had raised and turn it into a better experience for our clients.

"This Is Real, by the Way . . ."

Several hours into a leadership training session with an airport operations organization going through major changes, I asked the group, "What big organizational change that's been decided is your group struggling with and caught in resistance about?"

The groan that arose was so synchronized it might have been rehearsed. Nearly two hundred leaders were in immediate agreement: "The software update." Without prompting, they offered reasons why the update was a bad idea. It hadn't been thoroughly thought through, people said, and it was terrible timing for the business.

One frustrated employee was the most heated among seven others at his table. He was certain this update would never work, and he argued they shouldn't have to invest time in trying. Several others were convinced the IT group had hatched the software update with the sinister motive of making everyone's work life an absolute nightmare. Still others chimed in: Senior leaders would have known that it was a bad decision if they'd consulted employees beforehand.

The "why we can't" energy had flared up and continued to build. This was an example of resistance to change or, at the very least, lack of clarity about why a decision was made by the organization. It was clear most of the group had no desire to move to next right action to deliver on what the organization now needed.

I knew it was a perfect time to use the Negative Brainstorming tool.

First, we confirmed with the technology department that the software update decision could not be altered or scuttled. I turned to the flip chart and, at the top, wrote "CHANGE: SOFTWARE UPDATE." Underneath, I wrote "ISSUES."

After validating the team's experience that there was some uncertainty out there and that it could be scary for some, I encouraged the group to get as negative as they could about the software update. What exactly was keeping them from embracing this decision and buying in to execute it smoothly? After exhausting their issues, I confirmed they felt complete in sharing their worries.

After thanking them for sharing, I crossed out "ISSUES" on the flip chart and relabeled the list "RISKS."

CHANGE: SOFTWARE UPDATE		
~~ISSUES~~ RISKS	PROBABILITY	IMPACT
Lack of training		
Not all hardware supports the new software		
Some machines are too old		
Rolling this out during our busiest season—terrible timing		
Project scope keeps growing		
Changing workflows are involved		
People don't even know it is happening yet		
IT never finishes these rollouts in time		
No backup plan if it crashes		

CHANGE: SOFTWARE UPDATE		
~~ISSUES~~ RISKS	PROBABILITY	IMPACT
Something could break that is critical in our current setup		
There are old files and programs that only work in the old system		

Immediately, the energy and body language in the room shifted. An individual who had been particularly vocal about why the software update was a horrible idea leaned back in his chair, crossed his arms, and refused to participate. Other folks, who had tuned out and become slightly overwhelmed during the listing of concerns, leaned forward and began assessing the risks with newfound curiosity. Now that the energy had shifted toward "how we could," the highly accountable individuals felt liberated to reengage and participate. As the group assessed probability and impact, one critical concern was highlighted: "No training on this new software update." The issue of risk became a point of contention.

I asked folks who voted *low risk* to clarify. One voter replied, "My role in the organization happens to be coordination of training and development, and I know it's low risk because we have training set up. It's on everyone's calendar for Thursday of next week, and it looks like 99 percent are signed up." He turned to the man who had emphatically argued that the training issue was high probability and high impact in hindering the success of the change. "Ricky, did you to see that email we sent out a few days ago for training?"

In that instant, we had discovered the remaining 1 percent who hadn't signed up for training.

The Negative Brainstorming tool revealed a personal development opportunity for Ricky, because guess what Ricky often neglected to do? Read his email.

In fact, a few colleagues knew that he had an automated rule set up in his inbox that all training emails be redirected to his trash folder! In this moment, the tool showed Ricky's legitimate concern had already been addressed, and the exercise became a subtle yet public *personal* call to greatness for him. The leader wasn't calling him out; the Negative Brainstorming tool exposed the root of his resistance.

This is the power of Negative Brainstorming. In this case, it revealed the lack of willingness of some individuals to do what the organization needed to succeed.

The interaction was eye-opening and insightful, but to keep peace, I labeled the risk *medium*. Ricky's resistance de-escalated, and the group quickly finished the process for the remaining probability and impact for each risk.

By the end of the exercise, the Negative Brainstorming tool surfaced the lack of clarity and resistant energy and created a place to channel negative input and express legitimate concerns. Here is a recreation of where the tool ended up:

~~ISSUES~~ RISKS	PROBABILITY	IMPACT
Lack of training	M	H
Not all hardware supports the new software	M	M
Some machines are too old	M	L
Rolling this out during our busiest season—terrible timing	L	L
Project scope keeps growing	M	M
Changing workflows are involved	H	H
People don't even know it is happening yet	L	L
IT never finishes these rollouts in time	L	M
No backup plan if it crashes	L	M

~~ISSUES~~ RISKS	PROBABILITY	IMPACT
Something could break that is critical in our current setup	L	L
There are old files and programs that only work in the old system	M	H

The process helped the group get intentional about their thinking and prioritize which risks would be best to start with. The group agreed to cross out anything that was *low–low* or *medium–low* for now and focus on the higher-probability and higher-impact concerns. With the three items circled above, I posed the next question baked into the tool: "Given these risks, what are three things we can do to mitigate each one?"

After some additional silence, I could see the wheels turning in people's heads. Eventually, the group began to speak, and the ideas flowed toward solutions and possibilities. By the end of the exercise, the most concerning risks now had practical actions that could be started that afternoon to ensure a higher likelihood of success.

Once we had all the proposed solutions down, it was time to take all the work from the tool and ensure that it moved into action. Remember, if a tool doesn't end with who, doing what, by when, then the call to greatness never happened.

We asked the group, "Who would like to take action on these?" Then we assigned each task with an expected due date.

Frustration with the IT department had simmered down, and resistance was defused. The tool created a written record of the commitments and who, doing what, by when. The energy shift created by the tool was so profound that the head of IT grabbed the microphone as we headed out to a break and announced to the entire group, "This was real, by the way . . ."

At the conclusion of the half-hour exercise, the group that had metaphorically carried torches and pitchforks with an intent to destroy the change could see that the update was necessary and doable. Team members were now among the willing, and leaders used this experience and tool to regroup and move through other change initiatives in the organization.

Months later, the entire IT leadership and the participants who had experienced the tool together sent an email expressing gratitude. They told us that one tool had single-handedly cleared the fog of resistance that had plagued many previous projects. Most important, they used the tool as their secret weapon to navigate all fear, anxiety, and resistance to change moving forward.

We Solved Seven Issues by Doing Nothing

In another instance, Negative Brainstorming provided immediate relief to overwhelmed leaders in a large health-care organization. I was facilitating a session with a group of health-care leaders who had identified an organizational decision that was experiencing serious pushback: an overhaul to the Electronic Health Record system.

Such systems are standard in the health-care industry, using software to create efficiency and standardization to better serve patients. But in the early stages of implementation, people in the organization were experiencing lack of clarity and widespread resistance.

After validating the group's experience that large-scale changes can be challenging, I also empathized with their frustration. Many people seemed to believe there was too much going on in the organization to fully embrace this latest change. Earlier in the day, we had cleaned up some thinking with the Edit Your Story tool, spent some time finding our part in where the change was stuck with the Accounting For tool, and had just closed our discussion on the roles available in working toward a solution. Even so, this group was still stuck in resistance and having trouble seeing a path to next right action. I used Negative Brainstorming to invite the group to openly share their concerns and unspoken worries that were causing them to dig their heels in instead of embracing this mandatory change that had already been decided.

Tension built as I listed "ISSUES" on the flip chart. About six people enthusiastically called out issues and concerns, but most were silent. The final list had thirty issues across four flip chart pages.

When it was complete, I scanned the room and noticed, with shock, that a few participants had fallen asleep! Some people were so disinterested in *the most urgent issue in their organization* that napping seemed a better use of their time. Another large chunk of the audience seemed overwhelmed by the negativity from people sharing the "why we can't move this forward" issues.

As before, when I crossed out "ISSUES" for "RISKS," the mood shifted, revealing the skeptical and the willing. People from the resistant group leaned back in their chairs, crossed their arms, and smirked. Those who had been frustrated by the resistance looked as if they had just seen a sliver of light in a sea of darkness and seemed to lean forward, excited to get back involved. Our sleepers kept sleeping.

Three themes emerged during the exercise. First, the Negative Brainstorming list made it clear that the organization's decision was not negotiable and already decided. The investment in the project had been made. Second, during the risk probability and impact exercise, those who had been active in calling out concerns went silent. Third, the willing individuals who were high in accountability were highly engaged in formulating plans to make the initiative happen more smoothly.

The biggest breakthrough came from a nurse leader in the front row. She had stayed silent throughout most of the exercise, and after I crossed off seven of the thirty risks on the list assessed as low probability and low impact, she let out an alarmingly loud sigh. People began laughing. I asked, "Would you be willing to share what caused that spontaneous response?"

She said, "I was about to have a panic attack about how hard and messy this change was going to be, and now that you've crossed out those seven items, it feels doable. We have eliminated seven items on the list *without doing anything*. Before, we seemed so divided, and now it looks like we have clarity and a plan."

The Negative Brainstorming tool held the center in the face of resistance, built alignment around a necessary organizational change, and called out the most negative voices for their unhelpful behavior. Additionally, the people at the two tables who had been the most resistant knew what contributions would be helpful in future meetings.

Instead of every change announcement becoming an open venue for them to vent, complain, or point out all the problems associated with the decision, those individuals would now be invited to capture their concerns in the Negative Brainstorming tool and work with their colleagues to problem-solve and move forward given those challenges. For years, the people at those two tables thought it was most helpful to play devil's advocate in a cynical way and use their input to drill down on why something wouldn't work or why it shouldn't be happening. But now, they were clear on how to channel that same input into making it work.

Most important, the visual Negative Brainstorm had clarified where best to start in executing the change, with next right actions assigned to team members in the room.

Negative Brainstorm as a Decision-Making Tool

A leader in a software company shared with me in a session that he had $80 million in decision-making authority, but because he had to run everything through a committee, he couldn't make decisions quickly. Though the requests were typically approved, the process was tedious, time consuming, and frustrating. He realized his "decision-making" had serious constraints and wanted to address his unpreferred reality. Negative Brainstorming became his secret weapon.

Instead of getting stuck in frustration when the committee had concerns, he captured them as issues on a flip chart or in his notebook during their meetings. After the meeting, he used the Negative Brainstorming tool to assess the probability and impact of the concerns and worked with his team to formulate a plan to address those concerns. Together, they created action plans to navigate the biggest identified risks and added information about why other issues were low probability and low impact.

By presenting this new information to the committee visually, the exercise alleviated many of the committee members' concerns. Decision-making became more efficient and less frustrating. Most important, this leader discovered a magical tool to effectively collaborate with a board or committee and even looked forward to the feedback from those meetings instead of dreading them.

Remember, this tool cannot be done verbally because ego will work tirelessly to overcomplicate the pathway to next right action, especially when a group is faced with change. The visual nature of the Negative Brainstorming tool helps ensure that people move through change in the least disruptive and most productive way.

Even When It Doesn't Work, It Delivers

Sometimes the Negative Brainstorming tool works even when it feels like it didn't.

That was the case for our RBL team, which was feeling anxious about deadlines for an upcoming book launch a few years back. With competing work priorities and a request from our founder to secure additional marketing opportunities and create buzz around the book, we had a meeting to generate ideas, but it had become quiet and stale. Although our team was traditionally quick to problem-solve and come up with innovative ideas, in this particular unpreferred reality, we found ourselves stuck for our next right action.

As a few team members uncharacteristically shut down ideas that seemed reasonable on the surface, the meeting's energy began to slide into "why we can't" and "why we shouldn't have to."

"Why didn't we start this work months ago?" someone asked, which opened the window for an argument with reality. A few of us called out that it wouldn't be productive in this meeting to go back and forth about what we should have done up to this point. The fact that we were on a tight deadline wasn't the reason we couldn't succeed but was the new reality in which we must.

The team suggested funneling our concerns through the Negative Brainstorming tool to help get us unstuck. After acknowledging our unpreferred reality of being slightly behind and restating our founder's request and the approaching deadline, I grabbed a marker and went to the flip chart on the wall and listed several issues already shared:

- Not enough resources
- Too few team members
- Limited time
- Too many competing priorities
- The book publisher isn't landing us spots on blogs, podcasts, and other PR opportunities

When the group fell silent, I said, "Given this reality, let's get clear about the probability and impact of each of these risks on the success of this book launch." I felt like a hero, thinking I had revealed the pathway to help us reprioritize and create a concrete plan to succeed despite the circumstances.

Two team members went completely silent. They leaned back in their chairs and looked at me with the proverbial stink eye. I had used this tool successfully with countless clients, so why wasn't it working on my own team?

I thought maybe they were simply marinating in self-reflection, so I let the silence do its work. But still no responses came forward from the team.

I thought maybe the team hadn't heard me correctly, so I repeated the question, this time selecting one of the risks to be mitigated and getting more specific. "Given we have limited time until the book launch and are short of our goal, what are three ideas we have to mitigate the risk?"

Even more silence.

I decided to switch approaches and try to get the ball rolling myself with the group, so I said, "I have an idea; would you like to hear it?" Sometimes if you can throw one idea out in front of the group, it leads to a second, and so on.

I began, "We could rearrange priorities as we approach the deadline. Two of us are still heavily involved in supporting the upcoming public seminar event we have in a few months. We could pull those two team members to support the PR project for the book."

In my experience, this nudge and offering of the first idea will pop off the lid and enable ideas to start flowing. A few suggestions came in from other team members who already had a lot on their plate, but the two team members who had begun the brainstorm cynical had sunk farther into their chairs and now had their arms crossed. Noticing this, I playfully asked each team member whether they had anything they were seeing or would like to add.

Another bout of silence and shake of their heads.

This became puzzling because I knew our team (and in particular, these two team members) had the skill sets to dig deep to work toward the goal set by our founder. I knew we had the ability to adjust our approach to overcoming the problem, which is what I offered with my idea to start reprioritizing. But what I didn't expect was that the problem being uncovered in this project was a fading level of willingness to do what our company needed.

And the truth is that leaders can only work with the willing.

Dejected and confused, I used my exit line, and we agreed to table the exercise for the day. I saw the experience as a failure.

After a few days, however, I realized the Negative Brainstorming tool had done its job. While I'd hoped to come away with clear written action steps, the tool had at least revealed the lack of willingness in a few of our team members to do what the organization needed in this moment.

In this case, silence revealed that we *may* have had adequate resources; *we just weren't fully using the resources we had.* In other words, we had two team members who were completely checked out and stuck in resistance to trying to take next right action given the goals of our organization.

Trusting the tool and playing out the Negative Brainstorming experience in that meeting led to tough, necessary conversations about what it meant to be aligned with organizational goals. We saw where some individuals had disengaged and continued to resist the decisions of our founder to chase the lofty goal that had been set.

With this insight, we resurfaced the Negative Brainstorming tool in the next team meeting to continue the conversation toward "how we could" from where my exit line had left us. One team member who previously wasn't participating reengaged, to her credit, and started offering ideas. The other remained silent with arms crossed.

Noticing this body language and continuing on, the rest of the team clarified which risks were best to focus on and forged ahead to complete the remaining steps of the tool, even with the quiet team member appearing disengaged.

In the end, the tool was difficult at first, but by pushing through, it led not only to the successful action steps for the final weeks of the book launch but also to insights about our team dynamics and necessary conversations on performance.

I had conducted the Negative Brainstorming tool hoping to establish our next right action for achieving the new goals for the book launch with everyone pitching in their efforts. Instead, the exercise led to clear conversations on where more buy-in was needed by the individual on our team who was revealing his lack of willingness. This insight helped our team take next steps to address this behavior and discuss the drain it had on our team's culture, meeting dynamics, and productivity.

This new clarity shifted the approach to improving future team meetings. To initially counteract this behavior, our office manager decided to respectfully stop inviting this individual to certain team meetings.

Eventually, he came to our office manager and asked, "Hey, why am I not getting invited to book launch meetings?" The manager responded by clarifying what professionalism and true contribution needed to look like in those meetings and why participation in the "how we could" tools was critical to the team's success. This repeated unhelpful behavior given those clear expectations led to this individual realizing that the new strategies, decisions, and shifted responsibilities in his role no longer aligned with what he wanted, and he eventually transitioned off the team.

The Negative Brainstorming tool had acted as the spark to reveal a deep underlying lack of willingness and alignment and, with this employee's departure, cleared a drag of resistance and negativity that had been hard to navigate for quite some time.

The takeaway here is that although on the surface it seemed as if

Negative Brainstorming wasn't effective because of the lack of progress toward our book launch efforts and goals set by our founder, uncovering the underlying lack of willingness and resistance that had been tough to put our finger on within the team was the real breakthrough. For this reason, sometimes the tool works even when it feels like it doesn't.

Accessing the Tool's Full Potential

With a few examples of Negative Brainstorming now in your back pocket, let's cover a few critical reminders as you aim to get the full potential out of it.

- Capture issues on paper, on a whiteboard, or digitally on a spreadsheet, writing down concerns word for word if possible. The issues list can be as long as necessary.
- When listing issues, some people might feel overwhelmed or checked out. Encourage, but don't insist on, continued participation from all involved. Silence is also feedback. Lack of participation can be a great coaching conversation starter in their next one-on-one.
- Asking how to mitigate the identified risks can reveal whether the team lacks the skill sets needed, hasn't modernized their approach, or, most often, lacks willingness to take next right action.
- Always end with who, doing what, by when. Get a verbal *yes* from those assigned. Unless it's documented, it is as if the conversation never happened.
- If you're operating in the virtual environment, use platform tools, whiteboards, or a second camera or phone that points down to paper to make the exercise visual. You can also

download the PDF of the Negative Brainstorming tool with a tutorial video of how to do it at the QR code below. At the same QR code link, you can download the full Call to Greatness Framework Toolkit.

What to Watch For

If the ego is frustrated about not being consulted on the change or decision, it will do all it can to avoid participating in the Negative Brainstorming tool. Here are things to watch for.

- Be mindful that the first Negative Brainstorming experience can take anywhere from forty-five minutes to an hour, depending on the complexity of the change and the level of resistance. If you run out of time without completing all steps, express gratitude for the team's willingness to participate, and define a time to return to the tool in another meeting or huddle.
- For this tool, it is especially important to remember your exit line if the group gets stuck. Capturing all the fears, concerns, worries, and points of resistance and then relabeling them as risks to be considered is intended to transform the team's mindset—but it can also spark mental pushback. Once the design of the tool facilitates that shift into "how we could," some groups need some space and air to process before they can bring truly helpful input toward possible next right actions. For this reason, be sure to have your exit line polished

and ready. One exit line I like for Negative Brainstorming is, "Great work so far; thank you! We've made solid progress, and you've given me a lot to think about. Let's table this for now and move on to the next agenda item. I'll schedule a time to return to this."

- Be sure to remind people that "impact" is about the potential impact *on the business or organization*. Many participants want to focus on the impact on their preferences or comfort zones. Gently remind them they're not employed and compensated for staying comfortable and doing what is easy. A team's ultimate goal is to deliver on what the market, customers, clients, or patients require.
- In a rapidly changing environment, the results from Negative Brainstorming can have short-term effects. When new circumstances emerge after taking steps forward from the tool, or lack of clarity resurfaces or resistance reappears, then you've simply found a new opportunity for a fresh Negative Brainstorming exercise—or a full journey through The Call to Greatness Framework.
- Don't assume that silence means clarity or buy-in. Offer the Negative Brainstorming tool as a venue to voice any concerns or lack of clarity that needs thinking through. If no issues are brought up, trust that the team isn't holding back any unspoken worries and enjoy the lack of resistance. You have a team that is ready for what's next!

The Negative Brainstorming tool is also the best tool selection if you are sensing that your team or someone is

- Experiencing fear (of moving forward, failure, loss, repercussions, or even success itself)

- Resisting change
- Upset they weren't consulted on a decision
- Worried about the risks while moving forward
- Overthinking or in analysis paralysis
- Overwhelmed by the bigger picture
- Struggling to prioritize
- Focused on "why they can't" or why the team can't move forward
- Needing to share concerns before moving forward on a decision or change
- Wanting to test multiple ways to proceed and get feedback on how risky or disruptive a change or decision would be (e.g., "What would happen if we did implement it?")

Using this tool after performing the previous RBL tools in The Call to Greatness Framework for clean thinking, accountability, and buy-in fosters an environment where people are consistently encouraged to act with courage and trust their expertise.

With your Negative Brainstorming completed, you and your team have it: next right actions given the unpreferred reality.

Trust them. Go forward with them.

While you may have completed this Call to Greatness Framework and achieved next right action on your current unpreferred reality, don't make the mistake of letting these tools collect dust on the shelf. New challenges are always around the corner.

Next, you will learn what happens after you venture forward with the clarity and next right actions you've acquired from completing the full Call to Greatness Framework.

CONCLUSION

Bringing It All Together and Nudging You on Your Way

You've now walked through The Call to Greatness Framework and mastered six RBL tools designed to help people step fully into their space of impact. While the framework follows a clear linear path, it becomes a powerful cycle in practice. Once you've guided someone to clarity on next right action for one unpreferred reality, they carry it forward until the next challenge emerges and you begin again at Step 1.

The Call to Greatness Framework moves people from "why we can't" to "how we could," revealing where each person must evolve, whether by updating their skill set, modernizing their approach, or renewing their willingness to contribute.

Many leaders ask me, "Do I have to go through the full framework every time I coach or lead my team through a challenge? There isn't enough time to use all the tools for every issue people are going through."

The short answer is yes, but only if you want the highest return.

The order is intentional. Without clean thinking, teams spiral out of accountability. Without accountability, they struggle to buy into their role and the organization's goals. And when their perceived next right action is taken from the wrong role, it too often becomes an unhelpful next wrong action. The real payoff comes from walking the entire path.

In every instance when someone is feeling or behaving as if they can't, each situation benefits from first validating the experience of the person struggling with their unpreferred reality. Acknowledge the feelings they are having. Love them up.

Then, with discernment, begin Step 1 of calling them up to greatness. Ensure that their thinking about the problem is clean with the Edit Your Story tool. Bring in the Accounting For tool to ensure they have found their part thus far in the issue. From there, walk through the Organizational Alignment and Buy-in Decision Table to ensure they know their role in moving toward a solution. Finally, from that powerful clarity, select the next right action tool that best fits, whether it's SBAR, Thinking Inside the Box, or Negative Brainstorming. What comes from those tools becomes the way beyond the drama into possibilities and "how we could."

However, with time, practice, and fluency with the RBL tools, sometimes you can bypass steps. Your team may shift unclean thinking and judgment-infused stories into neutral immediately in the moment. People will start to get a shiver down their spine when lack of accountability or blame enters the equation. Roles are immediately clarified through constant self-reflection about the role they are being asked to play in a situation. From this streamlined flow through the framework, they are quickly able to plug into and play in any situation to start adding value. This speeds the process and allows leaders to bypass directly into the RBL next right action tool needed when they or their teams get hooked, triggered, or stuck.

Think of it as an expert masseuse who completes the full body massage but knows the key to true relief is releasing that one nagging knot in the center of your back. This is the same idea as you use this book to lead. Find out where you or your team is stuck in The Call to Greatness Framework; then the tools help set you free.

As this becomes a quicker process, some of the highest-performing teams I work with that are proficient and coached consistently on The Call to Greatness Framework square up challenging circumstances and move directly to what I've started to call the power tool of Thinking Inside the Box. This tool is a fast track to the space for impact that connects unpreferred reality to action toward an ideal future.

When you use the framework in full, you don't just solve the problem at hand; you transform the way your team approaches every problem. That's the heart of the call to greatness, moving beyond the drama and into the realm of possibilities, even in the toughest situations.

The workplace reality is riddled with challenges that will tempt you and your team to avoid the space for impact. The next one is coming soon, but that is nothing to dread, resist, or fear. It is simply an opportunity to validate the experience or feelings and begin flowing through the steps and tools of The Call to Greatness Framework. In fact, you'll know when "how we could" is embedded into your team because they begin to look forward to the next interference or unpreferred reality, as it is simply another opportunity to move through the framework, with curiosity, to what next right action emerges on the other side.

Final Words of Wisdom

You may already be seeing countless ways for these tools to start evolving your teams, but before running off to do so, there are a few words of wisdom I find helpful for those just getting started on their journey.

- Always start with love. Love people up, then call them up to greatness. I once heard that rules without relationships will equal rebellion. I would add that "how we could" tools without relationships equal rebellion as well.
- Be careful about using these RBL tools for evil and manipulation. Examine your motive. These should feel like invitations, not mandates.
- Start with your most willing team members, and then try the easy converts after that. Don't start with the person who has been resistant for years.
- Remember, the tools are best experienced when they are visual. When possible, look at the tool together from the same vantage point. The tools generate a thought partnership, not a coaching moment. Keep the process conversational so it never has to become confrontational.
- I often say, "I wrote the book on this stuff, and I screw it up, but only daily." You will too. There are always mulligans and do-overs. Coaching through the framework is about progress, not perfection.
- If you missed a call to greatness opportunity, you can always begin again. Model the behavior of starting over and pointing out where you missed a leadership moment. I love to reflect over the weekend and come back the next week and invite a do-over by saying, "Hey, I reflected on our conversation last week, and I realized I have misled you. I got into sympathy and colluded with you, and I'd like to try it again. You walk in and be you again, and I will be me. Start the conversation the same, and I will show up better this time. Ready? Go!"

- The core goal of the tools is to hold space for self-reflection and cultivate personal accountability. A tool done messily is better than no tool at all.
- Be mindful that many learn these tools to ditch the drama and then accidentally start to judge others who don't get the process or tools. Judging the judgers is the ultimate form of drama in the workplace. Always remember the mantra of "stop judging; start helping" in all that you do.

Drama Is Everyone's Business

If you have drama in your organization, it is either because you hired it, you inherited it, you allow it, or you are it.

For many, hiring is not the role they've been assigned in their organization. Even so, everyone can be accountable for their part in reducing the detrimental waste caused by drama.

By understanding The Call to Greatness Framework and the concepts underlying the RBL tools you've learned, even if you do it messily and imperfectly at first, you can rest assured that you will be doing your part to carve away drama at work. Once you grasp these tools, there's only one thing left: Commit to using them consistently for yourself, your team, and your organization.

Said more simply—practice, practice, practice.

We know from decades of experience that consistent use of these tools creates transformational drama-free results. Even better, the more you use the them, the more others will instinctively use them too.

When leaders actively use these tools, they stop managing the work of people and begin managing their energy away from drama instead. Soon, those noticing the same work is becoming more effortless will be joined by early adopters and willing team members who will experience breakthrough results with the same challenging circumstances that used to stop people in their tracks. Momentum builds, the culture shifts, and the "how we could" spirit begins to shine inside the hearts and minds of everyone in the organization.

The call to greatness isn't reserved for one flashy or inspirational person or those who have charisma or authority over others. These tools allow anyone to help those who are stuck to clean up thinking, step fully into accountability, and surge into next right action in the role the organization needs them to play. Moving energy away from "why we can't" to "how we could" is everyone's daily responsibility, no formal title needed. Any employee can begin ditching the drama and turning excuses into results.

Many people yearn for empowerment at work. But the truth is that your career empowerment comes from stepping into the power *you already have.*

Throughout this book, I've covered many case studies from Reality-Based Leadership and the ways our incredible clients have evolved and modernized their leadership skills by using RBL tools. We hope you will keep in mind that these tools are timeless and support you in any situation immersed in drama. You can use them to manage the energy of your boss, supervisor, CEO, or board member.

You can even use these tools at home, for those unpreferred realities encountered by your parents, spouse, children, or other relatives. However, a word of caution based on my own personal (and sometimes painful) experience: While The Call to Greatness Framework can be a beautiful way to support struggling family members, keep in mind that at home, you haven't been hired to maximize the productive use of time and resources to deliver a return on investment to an organization. Use your discernment, and remember that sometimes, it's better *just to listen* with love.

BUT ALEX, HERE IS WHAT YOU DON'T UNDERSTAND!

Each day, I have the good fortune to share this work. As I speak to companies across the world, it becomes increasingly clear that the RBL tools in The Call to Greatness Framework are the tools of the future. Not only is the framework powerful, but it is an essential addition to your leadership approach if you want to solve the rapidly changing challenges of the marketplace.

Maybe your ego is chattering, "But Alex, what if people aren't receptive?" or "What Alex doesn't understand is that we have *this* dynamic going on, and The Call to Greatness simply wouldn't fit with the way our team operates."

Or perhaps you're thinking, "I'm not sure about where to get started. How do I start to take all this new information and apply it at *my* workplace?"

One of the patterns of life that I continue to notice is that until you learn the lesson, you always end up back where you started. To find next right action forward, you can benefit from this wisdom by going back to where we started in the introduction of this book: Thinking Inside the Box. First, let me validate your experience and feelings of uncertainty:

I can see why you may be anxious or unsure about how to get started. I get that. I almost always feel that way when trying something new.

Given your goal is to begin calling your team to greatness using the RBL tools and given your constraints or excuses for "why you can't," let's think inside the box. How could you move toward that goal?

Then, make the box visual.

Challenges or excuses in moving toward the goal	GOAL: Begin calling my team to greatness with RBL tools from this book	Challenges or excuses in moving toward the goal
My team is different from others Colleagues won't be receptive to my coaching I have too much on my plate and not enough time I don't want to come across as mean or uncaring *<Insert other excuses below>*	How could you . . . ?	My coaching won't go as perfectly as it does in the book's examples I've already been colluding and sympathizing with my team We work virtually, so I can't make tools visual The people I lead have more experience than me *<Insert any other excuses below>*

Keep reflecting until the answer appears and you can say, "I can see it!" or a pathway shows up as to "how you could" get started. From there, follow the simple instructions. Take next right action, and trust in that clarity.

Then, when the next unpreferred reality appears and you feel stuck, start again with Step 1—just like the leaders and teams in this book did.

If you aren't using the RBL tools, you aren't ditching the drama.

You've been called to greatness.

Now, go be great.

ACKNOWLEDGMENTS

They say you teach what you most need to learn. Over the three years it took for this book to come to life, that saying proved truer than I could have imagined.

While writing about helping leaders move their teams from "why we can't" to "how we could," I found myself facing circumstances that gave me every justification to abandon this project. It became almost comical how many forces of "can't" seemed to be conspiring to prevent me from sharing these ideas. The ultimate test was this: Could I live The Call to Greatness Framework I was teaching?

Turns out, when you have no choice but to practice what you preach, you either prove the work holds up, or you don't. You're holding the proof that it does.

And none of that proof would exist without my incredible team at Greenleaf. Their patience, understanding, resilience, and constant loving calls to greatness kept this book moving forward when every reason existed to let it fade away. Tess and Lee, I cannot thank you enough for providing the spark this book needed at a critical time. Working with you was effortless, and you found the perfect balance of taking my voice and ideas and elevating them to the highest level in every chapter. Your team are the ultimate pros, and I cannot wait to continue bringing big ideas to the world together.

Ana—There aren't adequate words in either language you speak that would fully articulate what you mean to me, our family, and this amazing life we've built. You are the only reason I'm able to do what I love with this work, and your sacrifices that support me chasing these big dreams are something I will always be grateful for. When I think of what I strive for in loving people up and calling them to greatness no matter what, I think of what you do with our colleagues, family, and friends (and let's be real, mostly me!) each and every day. It's been one heck of a ride in our first decade together, and we're just getting this rollin'! I'm so glad that on that street in Manchester all those years ago, I told you the six reasons I loved you . . .

Archie, Augie, and Alvina—To my three kiddos whose toys are scattered around my home office as I write this, my hope is that someday when you run into challenges of your own, the ideas in this book will give you guidance to move beyond any place you're stuck. Your smiles and perfectly timed interruptions to show me bugs or a random toy you rediscovered helped keep my sanity throughout this process. Everywhere you go in the world, there will be plenty of people focused on why something can't be done. My only hope for all three of you is that you lovingly, with immovable conviction, invite the questions, "Well, what if we could? I have an idea; would you like to hear it?"

Dad—For instilling in me the discipline to see things through, to not cut corners by caring about the little things, and to be intentional with where I put my energy. I appreciate the sacrifices you always made as I grew up, introducing me to new sports and opportunities that helped instill a love for competition, leadership, and the importance of being a good teammate.

Mom—For showing me how to chase dreams while staying present for loved ones, for proving you can do things others don't think possible, and for teaching me that a life's necessity is to let your hair down from time to time and to, every once in a while, crank up the music until the house shakes. Thanks for all the visits coming back as a red cardinal in the backyard as I wrote this book. It makes my day to see the kids yelling, "It's Grandma Shelly!" as you fly by. Don't think I don't feel your push as I take that final step each time I go on stage to speak.

Ryan—For my brother, who has offered up more pieces of wisdom than I could count—some of which could have made it into these pages if only corporate leaders were ready for the unfiltered edition. Thanks for always being my biggest fan and urging me to keep battlin' out there in the world.

Familia en España—*¡Os quiero!* It has been one of the greatest joys in my life to be welcomed into your incredible culture. You've become our place of peace, joy, and recharge.

Dr. Stuart L. Weinstein—You helped a five-year-old kid who had lost all hope and could no longer walk find his legs again. You showed me the true power of continuing to focus on possibilities when all signs were pointing to the circumstances being insurmountable.

Coach Larson—The leadership lessons you taught and helped ingrain in me growing up have helped more than you can ever know. Our deep talks on living a great life continue to shape the leader, husband, and father I am today.

Cy Wakeman—Thank you for the start into the world of speaking and leadership development and for the lessons along the way, even the surprising ones I never knew I needed to be taught to evolve to the next level. You taught me the true meaning of "enough" and helped me understand the patience needed to let a full call to greatness unfold.

The RBL team—Thank you for all you do to help our team that prides ourselves on being drama free to ensure we stay drama free as we collaborate with our clients.

Dan, Brian, Erin, and Tevyn—I learned from you that sometimes the most courageous thing someone can do is to follow the simple instructions right in front of them, even if the path ahead looks a little scary. Dan, I cannot thank you enough for believing in us from the moment we sat down together. While your expertise has been invaluable, your mentorship, well-timed wisdom, and willingness to share hard truths will forever be appreciated. You showed us that freedom was a possibility and then made it happen.

Loice—Thank you for being the most unexpected joy we've encountered since moving to Texas! Your love and support have helped our family through some of the toughest times we've faced. We are so grateful to have you as part of our family.

我们像家人一样爱你

Michael—There is not enough homemade sourdough in the world to repay you for your well-timed calls to greatness over the last few years.

Jake, Mike, and Scott—Thanks for always answering my random calls on the way to the airport to talk about life and share inspiration. Your wisdom is always welcomed and your continued friendship greatly appreciated.

And lastly, **all my incredible clients and Reality-Based Leaders**—You took a chance on the new kid with a big game-changing message he just couldn't help but share. You rolled up your sleeves, took the tools of Reality-Based Leadership and "how we could," and got busy using them. You applied them in some of the toughest workplace situations because, let's face it, you're taking on some of the biggest challenges in the world. It has been indescribably inspiring to watch all of you both issue and answer the call to greatness time and time again. It is an honor to collaborate with your teams who are literally building a better workplace and worldplace every day. Doing all I can to share ways to shed the drama so people's talents can come forward in their highest self is my life's work, and I'm committed to fulfilling it.

RESOURCES

Learn more about Reality-Based Leadership's keynotes, trainings, and development programs for leaders and employees, virtual courses, certification programs, books, assessments, and toolkit guides at www.realitybasedleadership.com.

Listen to *Reality-Based Leadership: The Podcast* for tips, techniques, and the latest ideas for ditching the drama and calling teams to greatness at work. Subscribe on your favorite listening platform.

Want to calculate your drama level? Download the automatic calculator and complete your Employee Value Equation now: https://info.realitybasedleadership.com/equation.

Want your first six tools to start ditching the drama? Get them delivered straight to your inbox by following this link: https://info.realitybasedleadership.com/toolkit.

Additional Books from Reality-Based Leadership

- *No Ego: How Leaders Can Cut the Cost of Workplace Drama, End Entitlement, and Drive Big Results* by Cy Wakeman

- *The Reality-Based Rules of the Workplace: Know What Boosts Your Value, Kills Your Chances, and Will Make You Happier* by Cy Wakeman
- *Reality-Based Leadership: Ditch the Drama, Restore Sanity to the Workplace, and Turn Excuses into Results* by Cy Wakeman

INDEX

A

accountability, 76–85
  Accounting For tool, 79–85
  essential factors, 76–77
  grasp of facts is not personal accountability, 79
  honest self-reflection, 78
  immunization against cultural virus, 89–90
  not dirty word; path forward, 78–79
Accounting For tool, 79–94, 214
  common situations for using, 93–94
  engineer recruitment story, 87–88
  function of, 79–80
  identifying what's behind good results, 91
  immunization against cultural virus, 89–90
  steps for using, 80–82
  TikTok story, 83–85
  unproductive or stalled moments, 92–93
active disengagement, 5
Agreement Trap pitfall, 35
airport software update story, 195–200
answering the call, 130–34
  FEAR (False Events Appearing Real), 130
  inaction, 130–31
  skipping to the next right action, 131–32
  taking the right action (step 5)
    airport software update story, 195–200
    book launch story, 203–8
    company TV show story, 166–69
    COVID office safety story, 172–77
    credit approval story, 149–50
    electrical enclosure shipping story, 146–48
    Electronic Health Record overhaul story, 200–202
    getting more sleep story, 162–65
    Negative Brainstorming tool, 133–34, 185–211, 214
    SBAR tool, 132–33, 135–54, 214
    technology conversion story, 142–46
    Thinking Inside the Box tool, 133, 155–84, 214

B

bank growth and modernization story, 121–23
blame and finger-pointing, 49, 66
  Accounting For tool, 79–80, 92–93
  engineer recruitment story, 85–86
  moving toward accountability, 76–78
  seesaw effect, 72–74
  Thinking Inside the Box tool, 133
  validation without, 33
book launch story, 203–8

C

calling people up (to be the best version of themselves), 23–25, 44–46
  cleaning up thinking (step 2), 47–69
    compared to finding your part, 79
    danger of skipping, 213–14
    dealing with uncertainty, 68
    dealing with venting, 50–53
    defined, 50
    determining the truth, 52–53, 59, 62
    Edit Your Story tool, 53–69, 214
    exit lines, 68–69
    finding reasons not to follow through, 67–68
    keys locked in car story, 64–67
    loving your boss again story, 58–61
    loving your job again story, 61–64
    SBAR tool, 139, 146
    son's cut lip story, 47–48
    TikTok story, 56–57
  defined, 23, 44
  finding your part (step 3), 71–94
    Accounting For tool, 79–94, 214

blame and finger-pointing, 72–73
challenges, 72–75
enabling, 74–75
engineer recruitment story, 85–89
heroics, 73–74
identifying what's behind good results, 91
immunization against cultural virus, 89–90
jumping into action, 72
personal accountability, 76–85
struggle with follow-through, 72
TikTok story, 83–85
unproductive or stalled moments, 92–93
knowing your role (step 4), 95–127
bank growth and modernization story, 121–23
confusing *what* with *how*, 123–25
danger of role ambiguity, 96–97
goals, roles, and procedures concept, 97–104
hospital monitoring system story, 116–18
insurance company transformation story, 124–25
Organizational Alignment and Buy-In Decision Table, 105–27, 133–34, 214
surrendering control of tasks outside your role, 119–21
TikTok story, 110–15
uncomfortable truths, 121–22
wasted energy and missed opportunities, 118–21
moving from validation to action, 44
need to love people up first, 23–25
sequence of steps, 45
thinking inside the box, 184
as transformational journey, 44
worldplace/workplace, 23
Call to Greatness Framework, 8–19. *See also* cleaning up thinking; finding your part; knowing your role; taking the right action; validation
answering the call, 130–211
anxiety over getting started, 219–20
avoiding appearance of harshness, 12–13
breakthroughs, 15
calling people up to be the best version of themselves, 23–25, 41–42, 44–46
consistency and reliability of, 16–17
downloading toolkit, 19
for everyone, not just leaders, 16–18
exiting early, 12
foundational relationship, 22
increased fluency in, 13
initial clarity versus optimal clarity, 12, 45, 55
intellectualizing the framework, 45
as invitation, 9, 216
living within team's mindset, 17
loving people up, 22–25, 216, 218
missed opportunities, 118–21, 216
peer reinforced, 18
replication, 17
shift from "why we can't" to "how we could," 17, 19, 37, 213–18
skimming the growth opportunity, 45
skipping steps, 12–13, 31, 45, 131–32, 213–14
steps of, 9
stuck points (knots), 13–14
touch-and-go approach, 12, 37–38, 56
unpreferred realities, 9–11
visual versus verbal tools, 14–16
whole greater than parts, 12
clarity
about goals, 98
about procedures, 103
about roles, 96–97, 117, 130
Edit Your Story tool, 55, 72
initial versus optimal, 12, 45, 55
Know Your Role tool, 104–5
moving from initial clarity to action steps, 60–61, 72
Negative Brainstorming tool, 190, 210
Organizational Alignment and Buy-In Decision Table, 105
SBAR tool, 139
cleaning up thinking (step 2), 47–69
compared to finding your part, 79
danger of skipping, 213–14
dealing with uncertainty, 68
dealing with venting, 50–53
defined, 50
determining the truth, 52–53, 59, 62
Edit Your Story tool, 53–69, 214
action ideas, 55–56
dealing with uncertainty, 68
engineer recruitment story, 87
exit lines, 68–69
finding reasons not to follow through, 67–68
function of, 53
initial clarity versus optimal clarity, 55, 72
steps for using, 54–55
exit lines, 68–69
finding reasons not to follow through, 67–68
keys locked in car story, 64–67
loving your boss again story, 58–61
loving your job again story, 61–64
SBAR tool, 139, 146
son's cut lip story, 47–48
TikTok story, 56–57
commitment
to changes, 88

personal accountability mindset, 76
company TV show story, 166–69
consultant role, 101–2, 117
continuous learning
Accounting For tool, 82
personal accountability mindset, 77
thought partnership, 146
COVID office safety story, 172–77
credit approval story, 149–50
credit card sign-up story, 1–4, 19

D

decision-maker role, 100–102, 117, 119–20, 149–50, 182
Deloitte, 5
disengagement, 5, 10, 19, 206–7
drama
defined, 1
ego-based thinking and behaviors, 49
as everyone's business, 217–18
focus on ditching, 6–8
as mental/emotional waste, 6–7
role identification, 96
self-reflection, 50
using tools to ditch, 7–8
validating, 32
Whac-A-Mole approach, 12, 14
Dreaded One-Upper pitfall, 36

E

Edit Your Story tool, 53–69, 214
action ideas, 55–56
dealing with uncertainty, 68
engineer recruitment story, 87
exit lines, 68–69
finding reasons not to follow through, 67–68
function of, 53
initial clarity versus optimal clarity, 55, 72
keys locked in car story, 66–67
loving your boss again story, 58–61
loving your job again story, 62–64
steps for using, 54–55
TikTok story, 56–57
ego-based thinking and behaviors, 48–51
Accounting For tool, 92
cleaning up thinking, 50
confidence versus ego, 49
Edit Your Story tool, 53, 55, 68
judger and creator, 49
keys locked in car story, 64–67
Negative Brainstorming tool, 203, 209
Organizational Alignment and Buy-In Decision Table, 125–26
SBAR tool, 151–52
using tools verbally, 180, 203
venting, 50–51
war against happiness, 15
Einstein, Albert, 71
electrical enclosure shipping story, 146–48
Electronic Health Record overhaul story, 200–202
emotions
acknowledging, 32, 36–37
emotional waste of drama, 6–7
regulation as sign of sufficient validation, 38–39
empathy, 18–19, 28–32
choosing over sympathy, 31
choosing sympathy over, 30
emergency department example, 28–29
sympathy versus, 28–29
engineer recruitment story, 85–89
Eubank, Maximilian, ii
exit lines, 68–69, 206, 209–10

F

FEAR (False Events Appearing Real), 130
finding your part (step 3), 71–94
Accounting For tool, 79–94, 214
common situations for using, 93–94
function of, 79–80
identifying what's behind good results, 91
steps for using, 80–82
unproductive or stalled moments, 92–93
blame and finger-pointing, 72–73
challenges, 72–75
enabling, 74–75
engineer recruitment story, 85–89
heroics, 73–74
identifying what's behind good results, 91
immunization against cultural virus, 89–90
jumping into action, 72
personal accountability, 76–85
struggle with follow-through, 72
TikTok story, 83–85
unproductive or stalled moments, 92–93
Fixing Reflex pitfall, 35–36
flow state (the zone), 9

G

Gallup, 4–5
getting more sleep story, 162–65
goals, roles, and procedures concept, 97–104
dangers of ambiguity, 97–98
goals, 98–99
procedures, 103–4
roles, 99–103
Good Person to Be Informed role, 101–2, 117, 119–20

H

heroics, 36, 73–74, 93
hospital monitoring system story, 116–18

I

insurance company transformation story, 124–25

J

judging the judgers, 217

K

Katie, Byron, 15
keys locked in car story, 64–67
knowing your role (step 4), 95–127
  bank growth and modernization story, 121–23
  confusing *what* with *how*, 123–25
  danger of role ambiguity, 96–97
  goals, roles, and procedures concept, 97–104
  hospital monitoring system story, 116–18
  insurance company transformation story, 124–25
  Organizational Alignment and Buy-In Decision Table, 105–27, 133–34, 214
    common situations for applying, 126–27
    confusing *what* with *how*, 123–25
    function of, 105
    steps for using, 105–10
    tips for using, 125–26
    uncomfortable truths revealed by, 121–22
surrendering control of tasks outside your role, 119–21
TikTok story, 110–15
uncomfortable truths, 121–22
wasted energy and missed opportunities, 118–21

L

language shifts, 38–39
leadership. *See also* answering the call; calling people up; loving people up
  alarming trends in, 4–6, 19
  avoiding appearance of harshness, 12–13
  circumstances as reality, not reason, 4
  clear, repeatable way to use tools, 7–8
  confusing leaders with problem, 15–16
  core responsibilities, 23
  current approach is unsustainable, 6
  disengagement, 5
  empathy, 29–31
  energy management, 11
  focus on ditching drama, 6–8
  framework for, 17–18
  misguided connection, 28–29
  power in getting people to think/reflect, 9
  preferred versus unpreferred reality, 9–10
  value in navigating the imperfect, unpredictable, chaotic, 10
Life's Messy, Live Happy (show), 166–69
loving people up, 22–25
  broad definition, 23
  importance of as first step, 23–25
  listening, 218
  as necessity before calling people up first, 23–25, 216
  Organizational Alignment and Buy-In Decision Table, 122, 126
  specific definition, 23
  thinking inside the box, 184
  validation, 33, 40
Loving What Is (Katie), 15
loving your boss again story, 58–61
loving your job again story, 62–64

M

martyr role, 30, 74

N

Negative Brainstorming tool, 133–34, 185–211, 214
  airport software update story, 195–200
  book launch story, 203–8
  common situations for using, 210–11
  for decision-making, 202–3
  Electronic Health Record overhaul story, 200–202
  fear and resistance, 184–85
  function of, 133, 185, 190
  issues to watch out for, 209–10
  steps for using, 187–89
  TikTok story, 190–95
  tips for using, 208–9
nonnegotiables, 103–4

O

Organizational Alignment and Buy-In Decision Table, 105–27, 133–34, 214
  bank growth and modernization story, 121–23
  common situations for applying, 126–27
  confusing *what* with *how*, 123–25
  function of, 105
  hospital monitoring system story, 117–18
  insurance company transformation story, 124–25
  steps for using, 105–10

TikTok story, 110–15
tips for using, 125–26
uncomfortable truths revealed by, 121–22
Overvalidation Loop pitfall, 36
ownership, 76

P

passive disengagement, 5
procedures, 103–4
nonnegotiables, 103–4
pressure to make exceptions, 103–4
projection, 15, 164

R

Reality-Based Leadership (RBL). *See also* Call to Greatness Framework; TikTok story
origin of, 1–4
overview of work, 6–8
Reflection Ruiner pitfall, 36
resilience, 76
righteous high performers, 74
roles, 99–103. *See also* knowing your role
clarity about, 96–97, 117, 130
consultant role, 101–2, 117
decision-maker role, 100–102, 117, 119–20, 149–50, 182
Good Person to Be Informed role, 101–2, 117, 119–20
versus job descriptions, 99
martyr role, 30, 74
surrendering control of tasks outside your role, 119–21
unpreferred realities, 10–11, 104–5

S

SBAR (Situation, Background, Assessment, and Recommendations) tool, 132–33, 135–54, 214
common situations for using, 153–54
credit approval story, 149–50
electrical enclosure shipping story, 146–48
function of, 132–33, 135–36
idea-gathering process, 150–51
moving from ambiguity to clarity, 139
patterns to avoid, 151–53
steps for using, 136–38
technology conversion story, 142–46
thought partnership, 139
TikTok story, 140–42
using as starting point, 133–34
self-reflection, 9, 16, 217
avoidance of and discomfort with, 39, 92
determining the truth, 52–53
Edit Your Story tool, 53, 62
personal accountability, 78
SBAR tool, 151
silence to promote, 164
Thinking Inside the Box tool, 164, 181
venting, 50
side by side, standing/sitting to look at tools together, 16, 126, 164, 171, 181, 216
Situation, Background, Assessment, and Recommendations tool. *See* SBAR tool
skimming the growth opportunity, 45
step 1. *See* validation
step 2. *See* cleaning up thinking
step 3. *See* finding your part
step 4. *See* knowing your role
step 5. *See* taking the right action
Story Expansion pitfall, 36
stuck points (knots), 13–14
sympathy, 28–31
choosing empathy over, 31
choosing over empathy, 30
emergency department example, 28–29
empathy versus, 28–29
phrases that sympathize and enable victimhood, 35
trap of, 31

T

taking the right action (step 5), 130–34
airport software update story, 195–200
book launch story, 203–8
company TV show story, 166–69
COVID office safety story, 172–77
credit approval story, 149–50
electrical enclosure shipping story, 146–48
Electronic Health Record overhaul story, 200–202
FEAR (False Events Appearing Real), 130
getting more sleep story, 162–65
inaction, 130–31
Negative Brainstorming tool, 133–34, 185–211, 214
common situations for using, 210–11
for decision-making, 202–3
fear and resistance, 184–85
function of, 133, 185, 190
issues to watch out for, 209–10
steps for using, 187–89
TikTok story, 190–95
tips for using, 208–9
SBAR tool, 132–33, 135–54, 214
common situations for using, 153–54
credit approval story, 149–50
electrical enclosure shipping story, 146–48
function of, 132–33, 135–36
idea-gathering process, 150–51

moving from ambiguity to clarity, 139
patterns to avoid, 151–53
steps for using, 136–38
technology conversion story, 142–46
thought partnership, 139
TikTok story, 140–42
using as starting point, 133–34
skipping to the next right action, 131–32
technology conversion story, 142–46
Thinking Inside the Box tool, 133, 155–84, 214, 219–20
clearly articulated boundaries, 157–59
common situations for using, 183
function of, 133, 159
losing argument with reality, 156–57
paralysis, 155–56
steps for using, 160–61
sucker's choice, 178–79
tips for using, 179–83
technology conversion story, 142–46
Thinking Inside the Box tool, 133, 155–84, 214, 219–20
clearly articulated boundaries, 157–59
common situations for using, 183
company TV show, 166–69
COVID office safety, 172–77
function of, 133, 159
getting more sleep, 162–65
losing argument with reality, 156–57
paralysis, 155–56
steps for using, 160–61
sucker's choice, 178–79
tips for using, 179–83
thought partnership, 139, 146, 216
TikTok story
step 1, 41–42
step 2 and Edit Your Story tool, 56–57
step 3 and Accounting For tool, 83–85
step 4 and Organizational Alignment and Buy-In Decision Table, 110–15
step 5
Negative Brainstorming tool, 190–95
SBAR tool, 140–42
touch-and-go approach, 12, 37–38, 56
2025 Global Human Capital Trends (Deloitte), 5

U

unpreferred realities, 9–11
arguing with, 10
as challenge, rather than other people as challenge, 16
defined, 10
ego-based responses to, 48–49
finding space for impact, 11
identifying how you got there, 77
minor, 56
next wrong action, 12
preferred realities versus, 9–10
roles, 10–11, 104–5
validating, 23, 31
wishing for different, 10

V

validation (step 1), 26–41
acknowledgement without reinforcing drama, 32–33
affirming struggle and agency, 40
authenticity, 31, 37
common pitfalls, 35–36
cost of misguided connection, 28–29
defined, 32
empathy versus sympathy, 28–31
enough validation, 36–44
examples of, 33–34
of experience rather than drama, 32
important distinctions, 32–33
keys to, 32–33
length of time for, 36–37
loving your boss again story, 59
loving your job again story, 62
moving from validation to action, 44
not skipping the human work, 31
phrases that sympathize and enable victimhood, 35
phrases that validate without colluding, 33–34
responding to venting, 52
sequence, 45–46
signals of sufficient validation, 38–39
suffering and trauma, 37–38
TikTok story, 41–42
touch-and-go approach, 37–38
venting, 50–53
determining the truth, 52–53
example of, 51
responding with validation, 52
visual tools
importance of, 8, 14–16, 216
temptation to talk rather than write, 151
visualizing goals, 99, 171

W

Whac-A-Mole approach, 12, 14

Z

zone, the (flow state), 9

ABOUT THE AUTHOR

ALEX DORR is a highly sought-after leadership development speaker, delivering more than 125 speeches annually for top organizations such as Bank of America, Mayo Clinic, Nationwide, Caterpillar, McDonald's, and the Washington Commanders (NFL), among others. Often described as "absolute gold" for leaders who want results, not theory, he is emerging as the go-to voice when organizations need timeless wisdom tailored to the business challenges of today. He holds the CSP (Certified Speaking Professional) credential, placing him in the top 5 percent of speakers worldwide, and was among the youngest to ever achieve that coveted award.

As CEO of Reality-Based Leadership, Alex envisions a world where work is effortless and teams are drama free. He holds an MS in international business from the University of Derby, England, and in a previous life was a professional basketball player. His favorite claim to fame? He averaged two points per minute against the Duke University Blue Devils. The problem is he only played for thirty-seven seconds.

When Alex isn't speaking or writing, he enjoys devouring his wife's sourdough bread and playing any and all sports with his three young children (and often whatever neighbor kids join in). Originally from Norwalk, Iowa, he now resides in McKinney, Texas.